Open My Eyes

And

Let Me See

Phillip J. Knox

Open My Eyes And Let Me See

Cover design by Paul McGowan
Quote "was blind but now I see" taken from the song Amazing Grace by John Newton

Unless otherwise noted, all scripture quotations are taken from the New King James Version of the Bible.

ISBN 10: 0-9802492-8-7
ISBN 13: 978-0-9802492-8-6

For book information or to schedule a speaking engagement, contact:
Phillip J Knox
Email philknox@bellsouth.net

Published By:
Evans Printing and Publishing
4104-C Colben Blvd.
Evans, Georgia 30809
(706) 210-1000

*It is with a father's love and a desire
to pass on a great inheritance that
I dedicate this book to my two sons,
Mitchell and Justin.*

*"...while we do not look at the things which are seen,
but at the things which are not seen.
For the things which are seen are temporary,
but the things which are not seen are eternal."*
II Corinthians 4:18

♥♥♥♥♥♥♥♥♥♥♥

About The Book Cover

After the first printing of this book, I had many questions regarding the cover. Yes, there is a message in the cover. In Technical School, my math teacher often told me, "There is a method to her madness." Therefore, I will explain my madness.

I bought the picture of the frog hanging onto the world and had the cover designed around it. It reminded me of some people I have met who viewed life just like the frog. They are just trying to hang on. You can hear it in their words and expressions; "If I can just hang on…."until the weekend, or until payday, or until retirement," and on and on. You get the point."

Even with "big eyes," we fail to see that God is working in our world today. We fail to see God in our normal day to day activities. So, my challenge is, "Don't miss God in the mundane. Look for Him; He is there!!!"

CONTENTS

Introduction

I believe God works in our lives every day and I believe that very few of us ever really see it. For some reason, we only look for God to work in the extraordinary; however, we fail to see His hand as He works in our everyday life! Why? We may think He is so busy running the world, He does not have time to be involved in our everyday life.

I have sometimes failed to jot down some of the truths of God's word when I recognized them. It is so easy for our minds to become cluttered and mingled into our everyday life so that the reality of God's word becomes lost.

This book is composed of 40 chapters. Each one is a short story of ordinary events from my life; ordinary events that have opened my eyes to see God working and His word come alive. I don't always see it, but at times, as I have read and studied God's word, over and over the truths of His word have been evident in my own life and daily activities.

These stories are very special to me and I hope they will be an inspiration to you in your relationship with Christ.

Open My Eyes and Let Me See…

The Frozen Pond

One of my earliest childhood memories was when I was about four years old. It involved my mother, our dog and myself.

I grew up on a small farm in a small rural Georgia community. I was the youngest of three boys and still at home with my mother while my brothers were in school. One particularly cold winter day, my mother and I went for a walk down the hill behind the house to our pond. I remember our bird dog Lady was walking with us. I don't really remember much about the type of day it was other than it was bitter cold. It must have been very cold for several days because when we reached our pond, it was frozen solid.

There's something neat about frozen ponds. I remember seeing pictures of people in the north ice skating on their ponds with all the surrounding landscape covered in a blanket of snow. This was never seen where I grew up. But to this little boy, our frozen pond looked like a winter wonderland. It looked like a place of beauty, of adventure and of excitement, but soon I would discover it was also a place of extreme danger.

All of a sudden our dog, Lady, ran onto the frozen pond. The ice held her for a while, then what seemed an eternity, but lasted only a minute or so, would forever be etched on my mind. The ice creaked, popped, cracked and...Splash! Lady disappeared. As quickly as she was gone, her head popped up through the hole in the ice. All I could see was her head and front paws as she frantically tried to pull herself up onto the ice.

My mother turned to me, grabbed me by the arm and snatched me to the ground, away from the edge of the pond.

She gave me a stern command, "Do not move!" and believe me, I wasn't about to.

Now my mother is frantically running around. Spotting a fallen tree, she runs to it, breaking off a large limb. Mom picked up the limb and ran to the pond's edge. She began to slap at our dog with the limb. I was horrified. Lady is struggling and I wonder why Mom is trying to beat her down? Mom kept slapping that large limb towards Lady and I began to notice something.

The ice began breaking. Eventually, Mom had broken a path in the ice to our dog. Lady swam through the broken ice to my mom and was saved. We rushed home and placed Lady in a warm bath of water, to warm her cold, shaking body then dried her with towels.

Throughout my life, my mind has wandered back to that scene at the pond's edge and one day it occurred to me. This is exactly what God has done for us; for we too were without hope and God sent His son to create a path for us to come to Him.

Friend, we must begin to view the cross as it really is. In our self-seeking sinful way, we find ourselves in a horrible, hopelessly lost situation; totally separated from God. Romans 5:10 says our condition towards God is, "...we are enemies of God." It goes on to say that while we were enemies of God, we were reconciled to God through the death of His Son and much more; saved by His life. Jesus even said in Matthew 18:11, "He came to save that which was lost."

Friend, this is great news! God is not trying to beat you down with a stick. You are already down. He has, through His Son, broken the ice to save those who are lost. Friend, quit frantically trying to do it on your own and trust in His finished work of redemption on the cross.

All Alone

In rural east Georgia, hunting was the thing to do. As the years pass by, I really have grown to enjoy bird hunting. I also cherish the time spent hunting with my children. One particular morning, I took my oldest son, Mitchell, who was eleven years old at the time, duck hunting.

We awoke before daylight and put on our warm camo clothing. We made sure our decoys and guns were in the truck. Finally, we put on our waders, which are rubber, vinyl or neoprene boots that come up to your waist or chest. They allow you to wade in the water without getting wet, which is very important when it's cold. We loaded up in the truck and off to the swamp we drove.

We parked at the edge of the swamp. While grabbing our gear, we noticed a problem. We only had one light between us and this makes for a tough walk through the dark swamp. Trying to share the light as best we could, we made our way to the duck hole through the trees, fallen logs, grass and stumps lying under the water.

After setting out the decoys, I led Mitchell over to a leaning tree, which made a great cover for him to stand near. Insuring he was set, I waded through the water to another spot, got myself set and turned the light off. I immediately began to relax, as I stood against a tree in the thick darkness of the swamp.

With a slight cool breeze blowing in my face and the trickle of water flowing past, my mind began to wander. I envisioned wood ducks falling through the trees with their wings cupped ready to land. I could envision a group of mallards circling over the treetops, spotting our decoys and ready to come in for a landing.

Slowly, my mind was awakened to the reality of the moment by a quiet whisper. It was like being awakened from a deep sleep; you hear something but it takes time for your mind to register the sound.

Through the thick darkness, I hear, "Dad are you there? Dad are you there?" Apparently, my young son was not having the same pleasant thoughts as dear old dad. I assured him with a whisper back through the thick darkness, "Yes son, I am here." That was all he needed to be sure he was not all alone. Suddenly, with a little smile on my face, my mind began to race trying to catch my thoughts.

Friend, have you ever had a time in your life, where the darkness was so thick, you felt you were all alone? As a child of God, you need not fear. He is there no matter how dark life gets and it gets extremely dark at times. He is there!!! In fact, He says in His word, Hebrews 13:5, "I will never leave you nor forsake you!" Also, He says in Psalms 145:18, "The Lord is near to all who call upon Him, To all who call upon Him in truth!"

Friend, this is God's promise to His children. Next time you find yourself in the midst of the thick darkness of life, and you will, open His word of truth and call out to Him! Friend... He is There!!!

The Lord Is My Shepherd...

As children, we often hear things we don't understand that seem to provoke our little imaginations to the extremes. Our minds began to visualize things we hear as bigger than life. This often causes us unnecessary fear, to over-exaggerate or to have overly excited expectations.

My mom, dad and I were talking and they both told me stories of their childhood, which are great examples of what I am describing.

My mom began by telling me that as a little girl during WWII, she had become extremely afraid. Her parents and several other adults were in conversation this particular day. During the conversation they began to discuss the problem they were having with these terrible and destructive armyworms.

"Terrible and Destructive Army Worms!" my mother thought. "Oh my! How horrible... Monster worms!" Her mind began to race. "How big must these worms be if they are in the Army?" As a little girl, mom lived in fear that these "humongous, monster Army worms" were going to come out of the woods and attack her and her family.

Later she learned that these "humongous, monster, terrible and destructive Army worms" were actually only about an inch long. In reality, the only reason they were considered terrible and destructive was because they would eat the foliage off the Bermuda hay fields. This left no hay for my grandfather to harvest and would create a shortage of hay for the milk cows in the winter months. We all had a big laugh and then my dad shared his story.

Dad, who was also a little boy during WWII, overheard the adults talking about the war. They would talk about how the American boys had to fight "guerilla warfare." This scared my dad to the bones. Gorilla warfare! He thought, "What wicked people trained gorillas to fight our American soldiers?" Dad said even the thought of gorillas scared him to death. What a big belly laugh we all had that day.

Have you ever heard the saying 'the nut doesn't fall far from the tree?' Later that night, I was thinking about my parent's stories and remembered one of my own. My parents are real Christian parents, not perfect but real, so I grew up in church.

I remember Sunday School, where we were taught scripture, how to pray and a love for "butter cookies." I still love butter cookies; you know, the ones with the hole in the middle that have flower shaped edges. I believe you could put a butter cookie on your forehead and your tongue would slap your brains out trying to get to it. I LOVE EM!!!

Anyway, as a little chap, I remember being taught Psalm 23. It begins, "The Lord is my shepherd, I shall not want!" I questioned why my teacher wanted me to say this. 'It's wrong.' I thought, 'She might not want the Lord, but I sure do!...And also those little butter cookies.' As the years passed, I learned what "I shall not want" really meant.

Friend, I was confused because of a misunderstanding on my part. God's word was right and true, I just didn't understand it. Sometimes in our Christian walk, we become confused and isolated from the body of Christ. This can happen because of a misunderstanding or a false teaching to which we have been exposed and struggle with.

Beware, don't let Satan use these situations as fear and discourage-ment in your Christian life. Friend, do not give up.

In Matthew 7:7-8, Jesus said, "Ask and it will be given to you; seek and you will find; knock and it will be opened to you. For everyone who asks receives, and he who seeks finds, and to him who knocks it will be opened."

Friend, you may not understand some things right now and that's okay. Just keep seeking!!!

And in the meantime, enjoy a few butter cookies!

Dad, I Love It

Fall of the year. The leaves are turning and displaying their brilliant accents of yellows, reds and golden brown. Don't you just love it? The beautiful sunrises, sunsets and slight northern breezes blowing in the cool autumn air will revive even the most dedicated couch potato. Yes, the dog days of summer are over and it's time to enjoy the outdoors again.

I found myself standing back watching my little boy and some other little boys, big-eyed and excited. The parents were all standing and waiting to get a glimpse of their little boy getting his football equipment, making sure it was the proper and right-sized equipment. Then, you see the boys showing each other the number on their jerseys…and so it begins!

Practice… night after night, drills, running, blocking, hitting, game plays, defense, offense and all us parents standing or sitting on the side, talking and getting to know each other. And my favorite time? Listening to my son's excited chatter on the drive home after each practice.

The big day… game day, nerves jumping, boys wide-eyed, coaches yelling and parents cheering, 'IS IT IN YOU?' If you have ever played or had a son who played, you know exactly what I am talking about. Does this bring you back to the smells, the sounds and the memories of years gone by? I didn't grow up playing sports as a child, yet watching my son's team and the thrill of seeing my boy out there on that field all dressed up in his football uniform, sure does bring me joy.

My son, Mitchell played tight end on offense. He would block or go out to receive a pass. I remember one play where Mitchell went around for a reverse handoff and it worked well for a big gain. However, later in the game when the play was called again, it didn't work so well.

The quarterback handed Mitchell the ball and Mitchell, running full speed, turned up the field. Bam! What a collision! The defense was on him. One kid hit him from the front and then another from behind; looked like a jam sandwich to me, with my boy in the middle. Then it seemed like all the other nine defensive players hit him and piled on top. Well, not exactly, but you get the idea.

I am thinking but managed not to yell, "Hey, that's my boy. Get off of him you bunch of overgrown rugrats!!!!" One by one the pile began to clear and I saw Mitchell jump up. So out goes my chest again and I am now thinking, "That's my boy, you show them!" Have you ever noticed how pride is short-lived?

Here comes Mitchell running to the sideline holding his hand. Off to the emergency room we go! As we are riding in the car, I am thinking, "This is it, he will quit and I don't really blame him." But in the quietness of the car, Mitchell holding a bag of ice on his hand pipes up, "Dad, I Love It!" Through all the ups and downs and even the pain that sometimes comes, he still loves it.

Friend, isn't it interesting that sometimes we let people we love hurt us; our spouse, friends, church family, children, parents and coworkers? Yet, we tend to linger at the table of unforgiveness. Why? We seldom think about how we hurt others and even more seldom how we hurt God.

Does God cling to unforgiveness towards us? Romans 5:8 answers this question. "God demonstrates His own love towards us, in that while we were still sinners, Christ died for us." Think about it. Even though we hurt God by our sins, He still showed His love for us through His death on the cross and His resurrection three days later.

Friend, if we know this love of God, how can we not love and forgive those who hurt us? Remember the old saying, "Unforgiveness is like eating a poison apple and waiting for the other person to die".

The news is my son didn't give up on football. So, don't give up on your relationships even though at times they will hurt.

The Wonka Bar

Charlie and the Chocolate Factory; what a great story! Willy Wonka owns a chocolate factory. He has no family and is getting older. Knowing he cannot continue to run the factory, he is in somewhat of a dilemma. What he will do with the factory is the question of which he comes up with a great solution. He is a very eccentric man who is very particular about how his chocolate is made and how his company is run.

He knows an adult would want to run the factory their own way, which would ruin the whole factory and the quality of his chocolate. Willy Wonka puts his brilliant idea into action. He places five "Golden Tickets" under the wrapper of five chocolate bars. Then he sends them in shipments of chocolate bars around the world.

The five children who end up with the five tickets will be invited, along with one adult to accompany them, to visit the chocolate factory. They don't know that Mr. Willy Wonka will be testing each one of them. He will be testing each one of the children to see which one can be trusted and trained to take over the chocolate factory.

It's a great story and I would definitely recommend the book and the movie staring Gene Wilder. As a family, we have a copy of the book and the movie and my youngest son, Justin, loves it. He has read the book and has watched the movie countless times.

One day Justin and I were at a local convenience store, when he noticed a chocolate Wonka bar. We could hardly believe it. Justin asked, "Dad can I get a Wonka bar?" Well what do you think I did? Of course I let him buy it...with his own money. Here is the great news. The wrapper had instructions to some kind of giveaway if the bar had a "Golden Ticket" inside. I couldn't wait until we got in the truck to see if he had won.

On the ride home, Justin just stared at the bar and I said, "Son, bust that thing open!" Justin replied, "No Dad! I want to save it and open it with Jacob." Jacob was my son's best friend in the whole world and is to this day. So Justin planned a night for Jacob to sleep over, because he wanted his best friend to share in the opening of the chocolate bar and hopefully the "Golden Ticket."

Justin taught me so much because he was willing to share what he had, asking nothing in return. My parents have taught me that in life there are two types of people; givers and takers.

Friend, are you a giver or a taker? We read in I Timothy 6:17-19, "Command those who are rich in this present age not to be haughty, nor to trust in uncertain riches but in the living God, who gives us richly all things to enjoy. Let them do good, that they be rich in good works, ready to give, willing to share, storing up for themselves a good foundation for the time to come, that they may lay hold on eternal life."

Friend, takers trust in uncertain riches. Givers trust in the Living God!
You know what else givers do? Don't miss this, it's found in verse18.
1. They do good!
2. They are ready to give!
3. They are willing to share!

I can almost hear the thoughts you may be thinking, "But I am not rich." Friend, you may not have tons of money and possessions, but if you have Jesus, you are filthy rich. When is the last time you shared the greatest riches of all?

Friend, Are you a giver or a taker?

The Spanish Gospel

I had a good friend at work named Thom who often brought us pastries and such, which he purchased from a local bakery. He also gave out many bibles to the guys at work. Thom was one of those guys with a giving spirit.

Several years ago, I went on short-term mission trips to Honduras. Many of the guys I worked with enjoyed hearing about the trips and Thom was one of them. The next time I was planning a trip, Thom came in with a stack of bible study booklets for me to take. They were the book of John and contained the scripture and study material; but the best thing was that they were written in Spanish. Thom said he wanted me to give them to the pastor of the church we were building. I set one aside for myself thinking I might learn Spanish one day. (Never did!) Isn't it amazing how God accomplishes what He desires and how He uses so many people to do it?

Anyway, years went by and my friend, Thom, had even moved and taken a job in another state. One day Les, my supervisor, had enough of the mess in our shop and demanded a shop cleanup. I started into my mess and in the process, found that forgotten Spanish bible study booklet. I thought about Thom and the pastor and congregation in Honduras. I placed the booklet in a bag I use to carry my bible and Sunday School material in. Now I have a short memory, so when I got home, I forgot to take it out of my bag.

The next morning I was off to work again. I carpool with two guys, Rick and Joe. We jumped into Rick's car and did our daily morning scripture reading and prayers. We have one carpool rule; the one driving cannot close his eyes during the prayer.

After the prayer, Rick, who was driving said, "My throat feels scratchy," to which Joe replied, "You need some hot chocolate."

Rick pulled into a convenience store right next to the Bojangles where we often stopped to get a breakfast biscuit. They both jumped out and stepped into the convenience store, while I sat in the car. I glanced over and noticed a young Spanish man sitting by the entrance to Bojangles. This was strange only because we had never seen a Spanish person at the store before. Then I remembered the Spanish bible study booklet in my bag. I quickly grabbed it and jumped out of the car.

Walking up to the man, who looked to be about 20 and well dressed, I asked, "Do you read Spanish?" He nodded yes and I held out the booklet so he could read the title. A smile came over his face and I said, "I want you to have it." I gave it to him, shook his hand and said, "God Bless!"

As I watched from the car, I noticed he never looked up, he just kept reading the booklet.

Finally, Rick and Joe came out with their hot chocolate. I said, "Look at that Spanish guy over there." They asked what he was doing and I said, "Reading a bible study on the book of John." "How do you know that?" they replied. "I gave it to him." I said and then told them the whole story starting with Thom.

Think about it, what did God put together for this young Spanish man to receive a copy of the Gospel of John?

1. Thom brought in the booklet.
2. I kept one, thinking I would learn Spanish.
3. Seven or eight years later, Les had us clean our work area.
4. I put the booklet in my bag.
5. I forgot to take the booklet out of my bag when I got home.
6. Rick had a scratchy throat.
7. Joe tells Rick to pull into a convenience store to get hot chocolate.
8. I happened to see the Spanish guy sitting in front of Bojangles.

9. I immediately remembered the Spanish booklet in my bag.

As we traveled to work, we were in total awe of God's plan and how He works. We kept looking but have never seen the Spanish guy again.

In the Old Testament book of Isaiah, we read, "For as the rain comes down and the snow from heaven, and do not return there, but water the earth, And make it bring forth and bud, That it may give seed to the sower And bread to the eater, So shall My word be that goes forth from My mouth; It shall not return to Me void, But it shall accomplish what I please, And it shall prosper in the thing for which I sent it."(Isaiah 55:10-11)

Friend, God will accomplish what God desires to accomplish! Let us pray He will use us and open our eyes to see His marvelous works.

Down But Not Out

In II Corinthians 4:8-9 we read, "We are hard pressed on every side, yet not crushed; we are perplexed, but not in despair; persecuted, but not forsaken; struck down, but not destroyed."

This passage reminds me of a family fishing story. Each year my parents, two brothers and their families, along with my family and myself vacation at the beach just below Tallahassee, Florida. We have a wonderful time, because the whole family is there and the beach is perfect for our personalities.

You can enjoy the beach, play in the water or sand, or fish, or clean fish, or cook fish, or eat fish and have a blast! No bungee jumping, no go-cart racing, no parachute jumping and no having to listen to whining children who don't get their way at some ride or event. It's the family, it's the beach, it's a fishing rod and it's simple! Well...sometimes!

Once, we got the bright idea of renting a charter fishing boat; did I mention a small charter fishing boat? Don't get me wrong, it was nice. It was a 24-foot center console boat but it happened to be small for this day.

Captain Coy worked very hard taking us where he felt the fish were, but the normally calm gulf was rough that day. The wind began to pick up and the waves became a little much for the small boat.

Our fishing party included my brother, John, my brother, Frank and his son, Cody, who was about ten, and then my son, Mitchell, who was eleven and myself.

We were all taking a beating on the ocean that day. I don't remember who went down first (got seasick) but I remember poor little Cody leaning over the side of the boat, looking like he was doing a jackknife dive, hugging one side of the boat with his legs and the water side of the boat with his chest. The best I could describe it was he looked like a paper clip jammed down tight on a stack of papers.

Frank, who never gets sick, was fighting the anchor in the front of the boat, when he turned a little green at the gills. He was trying to hold it back but he began to spew, looking like a fire hose on mist. John told Frank, "Let her blow son!" It was bad, real bad.

Next thing I knew, John is down and I don't mean just sick. He is lying on his back, on the floor of the boat, with one leg propped up on the side of the boat. At the time, we are over a spot where the fish are biting. I heard John tell Captain Coy to hand him a pole and bait it up. Captain Coy looked at me with a puzzled look on his face. I just shrugged my shoulders. Captain Coy, who was doing all he could to make this a good trip in spite of the bad weather, baited a pole and handed it to John.

What a sight! There is John, sick, flat on his back, leg propped on the side of the boat and holding a rod. I kept on fishing when I heard Captain Coy say, "That beats all I have ever seen." As I look around, I see Captain Coy wide-eyed with his mouth hanging open, staring at John while John is still on his back reeling in a fish. Frank, who was at this time back in action and fishing again said, "He may be down but he is not out!"

Friend, in the passage you read earlier, Paul points out a reality, that life will be tough. I don't know how this "feel good, everything is going to be good," and "the life of ease that awaits us Christians" preaching has crept into our churches, but God's word is clear, Life Will Get Tough!

It may be tough for you right now. You may be going through some extreme difficulty that has you flat on your back. You may not like it, it may not be fun, it may hurt physically or emotionally and you may not see a way out. But friend listen…listen…listen… as a child of God you may be down but you are never, never out!!!

Friend, take courage from God's word; lean on the scriptures, draw strength from His truths and when you do…while you are down, grab a pole. There are fish to catch! Remember, only when we are down and it is evident our strength for ministry comes from God, do people say "THAT BEATS ALL I HAVE EVER SEEN!"

Ask God to open your eyes to the opportunities of His work…even in the midst of your struggle.

How About A Hotdog

My wife's grandfather, John, is better known as Boompa. Boompa and Granny were a very neat couple. When you were around them any length of time, you realized they loved their family and that included me.

Boompa, like most people his age, grew up hard. As a young man, he began working at a local theater where he learned to be a projectionist. He also became very proficient at sound and theater maintenance.

Just like many other men, he spent time in the service during WWII. When he came back from the war, he went back to the theater business again. Later in his career, he was a troubleshooter for RCA in Miami, Florida.

Boompa and Granny lived on a small houseboat in the Miami Marina. Upon retirement, they planned to cruise their houseboat up the Atlantic Intracoastal Waterway. They had traveled past Daytona Beach, when his mother fell ill. Boompa and Granny decided to dock back at the Daytona Marina and help take care of his mother.

This is when I came into the picture. I married their granddaughter. Each summer, Terri and I would spend a week with them on the boat. They were always excited when Terri and I visited. Boompa would get his lifeboat out and put the sail on it for me to sail the Intracoastal Waterway.

We went to minor league baseball games, to the beach, shopping, out to eat, sightseeing and such. But when our children came along, the boat got really small, so we would stay in a motel, but this did not diminish our visits one bit for we always had a blast. Granny and Boompa couldn't wait until we brought their great-grandsons to visit.

Time passed by so quickly. Eventually Granny and Boompa sold the boat and moved up to Georgia to live near their daughter, which was about two hours from us. They still enjoyed our visits and especially seeing their two great-grandsons.

After sixty-six years of marriage, Granny passed away and now Boompa was all alone. I remember on Father's Day 2003, I called Boompa, "Hello Boompa, this is Phillip. We are coming down to take you to lunch. I am calling so you will be ready."

Boompa replied with excitement in his voice, "Come on, I will fix you a hotdog." I wanted to, but didn't... laugh, that is. I just said, "Get dressed, we will see you soon, goodbye" and hung up the phone.

"I will fix you a hotdog!" ... I had totally missed it. To me it was about taking Boompa out, feeding him a nice meal and doing something for him. But to Boompa it was about, Just Being Together!!! Boompa would rather have had 'us and a hotdog' than a big meal with all the hustle, bustle and distraction of a restaurant.

Friend, God is the same way. Remember Mary and Martha from Luke 10:38-42? Jesus visited the home of Mary, Martha and their brother. Martha wanted to fix Jesus a big meal, but Mary wanted to sit at the feet of Jesus. Martha got all upset and frustrated in her busyness; Mary was relaxed and renewed at the feet of Jesus.

Friend, maybe it is time to sit at the feet of Jesus. To be refreshed and renewed by quiet time with Him. Slow down friend...I believe if you called Jesus, he would rather have 'you and a hotdog' than the hustle, bustle and distraction of a big meal.

Purple Martins

Some things pass on from generation to generation. Have you ever watched the Antique Road Show? It's where people bring in old things and appraisers give them information about the items and the value of the items. Many times these antiques are passed from one generation to another.

Well, I inherited my grandfather's very own "purple martin pole." Before you horselaugh me to the ground... make sure you understand what I said. I did not say purple Martian (some purple form of an alien from Mars); I said purple martin.

Purple martins are birds. The males have a beautiful, deep purple color. They normally arrive to our area around late February and leave around late July. They are very protective of their nest and when they have young, they will dive-bomb at you to keep you away.

My oldest son must have been dive-bombed as a child, because he is still petrified of these birds. He doesn't know it but I already have the purple martin pole in my will to give to him. Anyway, the really neat thing about these birds is they eat mosquitoes and such. They are kind of like a natural mosquito repellant.

So my grandfather built a purple martin house to attract these birds. He took an old iron wagon wheel and attached it to a pole. Then he took dry, hardened gourds that he grew, cut a hole in them for a door and hung them on the wagon wheel for martin houses. So I find myself in the purple martin business, making sure each year the martins have new gourds to nest in. If you think about it, it's a good trade-off. I make sure they have a home to raise their young in and they keep the mosquitoes down for me. I admit I really have enjoyed the martins and hate to see them leave. As soon as they have left, the mosquitoes seem to no longer be kept at bay and come out with a vengeance.

Besides the purple martins that come each year, I have another "purple martin." His name is Lonnie. Lonnie is the godly Christian man in my life who helps keep the mosquitoes away. He is the person who will tell me what I *need* to hear not what I *want* to hear. He is the Christian friend who challenges me in my walk with Christ.

Do you have a purple martin in your life? You need one! I believe way too many who claim the name of Christ are afraid to have a purple martin in their life because they really don't want to change. We must get to the point where we want to hear the truth and then, desire to apply the truth. This is why I say, "you need a purple martin in your life." You need a Christian friend (of the same sex) to challenge your walk with Christ.

Think about God's word... Friend, do you have any purple martins in your life? In Proverbs 27:17 we find a very important truth, "As iron sharpens iron, so a man sharpens the countenance of a friend."

There is nothing worse than a dull knife...except a dull Christian!!!

The Fair Is In Town

Growing up in rural Georgia, you could say we were somewhat sheltered. Other than having a few neighbors and our cousins coming to visit, we played with each other. My brothers and I could always find something to get into. As a family, we would go to town normally once a week to buy groceries and such. I tend to be a homebody, so town and crowds were not my favorite.

I remember Mom and Dad taking us three boys to the Augusta Exchange Club Fair. It seemed to take days to even get there, though it was only about 35 miles. I must have been around age seven or eight at the time.

The fair looked so big and there were so many people. 'What if I get lost?' kept rolling around in the back of my mind. It was so noisy with all the loud music playing, mixed in with the sounds of the rides and millions of people talking. I did enjoy the lights; so many different colors and many were flashing. Each ride was covered in lights and there were lights displaying the vending trailers.

Vending trailers, the wonderful smell of hamburgers, hotdogs, vinegar fries, funnel cakes and cotton candy. Could there ever be a kid in the world who would not like cotton candy? My favorite part was walking around the livestock while munching on my bag of cotton candy.

But... I will never forget the games. Side by side, these games were set up; pop the balloon and win a prize, toss the ring and win a gold fish but what worried me were the people running the games. I now realize they were just making a living like everyone else, but they yelled at me. "Hey, you kid, come over here, step right up!" Bear in mind these people were not like my Sunday School teacher, or my neighbors or my aunts and uncles. They kept yelling, "Hey boy, come over here." I am thinking, "Oh please, let's just get out of here." This experience so affected me; I wouldn't go to the fair again.

When I started dating my wife to be, she was determined we would go to the fair. How stupid we men can be, well not totally. Yes... I took her to the fair. We went, got a bag of cotton candy and went to see the livestock while we ate it and then went home. For some reason, she never asked me to go to the fair again.

For years my two boys had been begging me to go to the fair with them and their mother, so at age forty I gave in. I had a wonderful time, nobody yelled at me and I ate cotton candy until it was coming out of my ears...or was that little hairs? Time to pluck them again! Anyway, I could not believe I had let a bad experience umpteen years earlier cause me to miss out on some great times with my wife and children.

Friend, has some bad experience caused you to miss out on the fellowship of God's family? Have you fallen out with the body of Christ because of some past experience?

In Hebrews 10:23, God commands us (Christians), "...not to forsake the assembling of ourselves together!"

Friend, I encourage you, if you are a fellow Christian, to be obedient to God's Word. Visit around to find a local body of believers. And, when you go in, do not look around until you have first worshiped God, then you will view others through His eyes and not your own.

Friend, remember you are hurting yourself and missing out on His blessings and some wonderful times if you "forsake the assembling."

Fireworks

There is something magical and mystical about fireworks. While you lie on a blanket and focus on the blackness of the sky, you suddenly see beautiful, sparkling, brilliant, colorful lights explode right before your eyes. The darkness is overcome and the landscape is illuminated as the explosion creates a beautiful display of colors. It's captivating, exciting and thrilling to say the least.

July the fourth 2005, my wife's grandfather, Boompa, came to stay with us for the weekend. We always had fun with him, but this was special because July tenth was his birthday. We would be celebrating July fourth and his eighty-seventh birthday.

I remember taking him to the grocery store with me. When we got there, I told him I was in a hurry and he needed to ride a motorized buggy the store offered. I am rushing through the store and he is on my heels in that buggy. As I am walking and thinking about what I had to get, I hear these words, "Look, no hands." I look back to see my wife's eighty-seven year old grandfather with a big fat grin on his face, the buggy is going full speed and he has his hands raised above his head. (Just like we would do as children on our bikes.) I had to belly laugh.

Every July fourth there is a celebration and fireworks display at a park about seven or eight miles from our house. The celebration starts early and can be described much like a carnival. They have kiddie rides, games, food and fun for the whole family. As night falls, they have a big fireworks show. This thing has become so big the police have to direct traffic. If you show up late, you have to walk a long distance. If you show up early you don't have to walk as far but you get stuck in traffic when it's over.

I live on a hill and as the crow flies, it's only four or five miles to the park. We like to sit on my back porch and view the fireworks as they explode above the treeline, which was perfect for Boompa. After having a nice supper, we all sat on the porch, waiting the start of the show.

Then it started. The sky began to light up with beautiful lights and colorful displays. The show normally lasted for about thirty minutes. About ten minutes into the fireworks, I heard Boompa, as he looked straight ahead at the show as if he was talking to someone particular, "I wonder if they even know what they are celebrating?"

Time out! Stop! Don't miss what he said. "I wonder if they even know what they are celebrating?"

Friend, are we guilty of the same? Can our churches become celebrations that we attend and feel good about, but do not know what we are celebrating?

Tucked way back in the Old Testament is the book titled Amos. In Amos 5:21-24, God says, "I hate, I despise your feast days, and I do not savor your sacred assemblies. Though you offer Me burnt offerings and your grain offerings, I will not accept them, Nor will I regard your fattened peace offerings. Take away from Me the noise of your songs, For I will not hear the melody of your stringed instruments. But let justice run down like water, And righteousness like a mighty stream."

Friend, these people loved to celebrate and they went all out in their celebrations. Why was God angry with them? Because they forgot what worship was all about and would not live like His people. They would not live in obedience to God. They enjoyed the celebration part but not the obedience part.

Friend, our celebration and worship starts long before we walk into the doors of a church. It starts with our recognition that we are not God; we do not call the shots, but we are willing to live under His authority and lordship in complete obedient fellowship with Him. My challenge to you and myself is that our Sunday celebrations will be an overflow of the love and obedience to Him, which we have shown to Him all week long.

What's On My Windshield

Ever get the feeling nothing is going your way? Life can be tough, no doubt. Since we lived on a small farm and enjoyed hunting, I decided to prepare a dove field so that I could invite several dads and their sons or daughters over for a dove shoot. This can be such a wonderful time of fellowship. But, it is hard to prepare the field for shooting dove.

On opening day of dove season, the best part is gathering for lunch and sharing stories, laughs and fellowship. Lunch was normally a fish fry with all the fixings; hushpuppies, french fries, beans, slaw, grits and of course, deserts. Then, it's off to the field for hopefully a good shoot.

It is great to see dads and their sons or daughters dressed in camo clothing talking and laughing. Fellowship is vital to a man's well being; in fact, God created us to fellowship with Him.

This one particular year was a disaster for me. To prepare the field, you have to mow the grass and weeds, normally using a bush hog. A bush hog is like a six-foot wide, extra heavy lawnmower, which is pulled behind a tractor. I was mowing the field, using my dad's tractor, which has a cab. I was almost finished when I heard a loud explosion and felt stuff hitting me on the neck and arms. The mower had kicked up a rock and somehow thrown it into the back glass of the tractor cab. The glass exploded all over me and inside the tractor cab.

Next, you have to plow the field. Where we live is "Rockville" or it should have been. I have a theory the rocks breed, every time you plow the field. Out in the hot, June Georgia sun my two boys and I picked up rocks, millions of them!!! The more we picked up, the more that showed up. I believe the wicked, evil rock fairies scatter rocks over the

31

fields at night. If you know how to get rid of the wicked, evil rock fairy, write me and let me know.

Then the planting starts. This is normally a fun time for me… except this particular year. Somehow I broke a brace on the planter, not once, but twice. It must have gotten stuck on a rock or root.

Once the planting is done, it's a matter of God sending the rain and making dead seeds come to life. Now there is a lesson in itself. Once the plants mature and produce seeds, the field is ready to cut; this is normally a couple of weeks before dove season. The seeds will fall to the ground and the plants are baled up for hay, which we feed to the cows.

My dad started cutting the field, and was more than halfway through, when I rode by to check on him. He had something to do so he asked me to take over cutting the field. (I should have played sick or faked being deathly ill.) But, I climbed on the tractor and began to cut hay. I only made a couple of rounds when a rock, that's right, a rock got caught in the hay cutter and broke some gears.

Oh Brother!!! I told my dad life was tough! He responded with his normal quick-witted humor, "Don't worry, it will only get tougher." I am thinking, "How?" I should not have thought that!

Well, I had a date with my wife that night. I washed my truck and had it cleaned up and looking sharp. Hot mama and I jumped in the truck. I mean she was looking hot.

Off to town we went. As we drove along and were talking, I noticed a mist on my windshield. What in the heck is this? I thought. I turned on my wipers and sprayed the wiper fluid and saw a cattle trailer traveling in front of us. And there in the cattle trailer was a big cow urinating and it blew all over my truck… Dad was right! Things could get tougher!

Friend, Paul says in II Corinthians 4:8-9, "We are hard pressed on every side, yet not crushed; we are perplexed, but not in despair; persecuted, but not forsaken; struck down, but not destroyed…"

How could Paul, having been through so many tough times, have this attitude? Paul gives us a clue as he continues on in the verses following:

Verse 10...that the life of Jesus also may be manifested in our body.
Verse 11...that the life of Jesus also may be manifested in our mortal flesh.
Verse 14...that we will be raised up with Jesus...
Verse 16...that we are being renewed...
Verse 17...that our tough times are but for a moment...
Verse 18...that the things we see are temporary, but the things not seen are eternal.

Paul understood what I learned at a men's conference. Life is Tough...But God is Good!

Press on my friend...Press on! Keeping your eye on the prize, God Himself!!!

This Water Is Cold

My wife and I really enjoy fishing. When Terri and I dated, she would go fishing with me. I figured that once she caught me, our fishing days would be over. But it's something we have enjoyed over the years so we decided to buy a bigger fishing boat.

We live near a lake and our boys were growing, so we purchased a used boat that would fit our budget. Terri would always fix a picnic lunch for us while I got all the fishing stuff ready. We would hook up the boat, load up the boys and off to the lake we would go. What wonderful memories we had on the lake.

For years, my brother had fished the lake and had become pretty good at it, so he showed me how and where to catch sunfish. (We called them shellcrackers.) The fish bedded in shallow water, usually around some sort of structure like fallen logs, stumps and such.

One particular trip, Terri, Justin, who is my youngest son, and I went fishing. It was a cool spring day; the sun was out with its beautiful rays beaming off the water and a slight breeze was blowing. We happened to find a large bed of shellcracker bedding and began fishing. Terri and I are catching fish left and right. We were using light tackle and these fish were giving us some great fights. My wife is a very godly, quiet, laid-back person but when she is fishing, a competitive edge emerges from somewhere.

At the end of the day, for a million dollars, I could not begin to tell you how many fish I have caught. Terri, on the other hand, will tell you exactly how many she has caught. So, here I am trying my best to get and stay ahead of her.

Justin, who was maybe ten or eleven at the time, is sitting over there doing his usual thing. He likes going fishing but does not fish. I enjoy having him with me, as he is a great first mate. He was keeping us in worms and, of course, playing games with them. He would toss our fish in the live well and made sure they had plenty of water. When we broke a hook, he would quickly get us rigged up again. There is a spiritual lesson here in case you haven't noticed. Not everyone likes holding a fishing pole but everyone can be and should be a part of the fishing!

Anyway, we are having a wonderful time. I had hooked a large fish and had one big fight on my hands. The fish won. It ended up with the fish right up under the boat, wrapped around a small pine sapling, just out of reach under the water. Looking over at Terri, I could see she didn't care, she just kept on fishing. Justin was looking at me.

Jokingly, I said, "Justin, get naked, jump in and get my fish." Then I got down and reached my hand into the cold water to retrieve the fish, but to no avail. Finally, I stood back up and as I did I heard, "Whoa! This water is cold." I look over and see my son, buck naked and going into the water. I could not believe it! Here I am joking with my son and his desire to please his dad led him into the cold water.

Friend, God is not joking and yet how often do we fail to please Him? He is our Heavenly Father and we are His children; yet, if we are truly honest, our desire is to please ourselves first.

We read in II Corinthians 5:9-10, "...we make it our aim, whether present or absent, to be well-pleasing to Him. For we must all appear before the judgment seat of Christ, that each one may receive the things done in the body, according to what he has done, whether good or bad."

This is a reality, we will stand before the judgment seat of Christ, but it should be our motivation to please Him and it should come forth out of our love for Him.

Friend, is your love for God so strong, your aim is to please Him? If not, go back and think how horrible your situation really is and how wonderful His grace is that brought you out. How could you not please Him who loved you so much? Get naked and dive in!

Death Row

Scott Peterson...who hasn't heard of his name? Several years back you could not open a paper or turn on the news without seeing some story about this man. Here is a man, convicted of killing his wife and unborn son. How can this be? Why? To be with another woman.

It's horrible and if you have watched the news at all, you know of this horrible story and how it unfolded. And what did he receive for this horrible killing? The death sentence! Scott Peterson was sentenced to death row...waiting to die.

When I heard this, I thought, "He was already on death row." Paul writes in Romans 6:23, "For the wages of sin is death..."

Friend, all of us, including Scott Peterson, are on death row totally separated from God. And why? Because of our sin. But wait a minute. "I really can't be that bad" is what most people think. The truth is we are! It doesn't matter what you think and it does not matter what I say, what matters is what the Judge says. So let's look. God says in his word:

- "The heart is deceitful above all things and desperately wicked," (incurably sick) (Jeremiah 17:9)
- "But we are all like a unclean thing, And all our righteousness are like filthy rags" (Isaiah 64:6)
- "There is none righteous, no not one; There is none who understands; There is none who seeks after God." (Romans 3:10-11)
- "All have sinned and fallen short of the glory of God" (Romans 3:23)

As we have read, no matter what we think, we are in a horrible condition. We have chosen to make ourselves #1 and

37

our sin against a Holy God has placed us where we deserve to be... on death row!

But God also has exciting news. Romans 6:23 states "the wages of sin is death," but it goes on to say, "the gift of God is eternal life through Jesus Christ our Lord."

Think about what happened; God sent his son and took your place on death row that you might have life. Not because He had to; not because He was forced to; not because you could demand Him to, but he died to give you life because, "He wanted to demonstrate His love towards us." (Romans 5:8)

Friend, All you have to do is repent and believe. You cannot do what only God can do for you. Repent, turn from your sin and selfish ways and turn to God. Believe that the death, burial and resurrection of Christ are a complete perfect payment for your sin.

Friend, I cannot convince you that you are on death row or to get off death row. But God's word can! Take time and learn for yourself the truths of God's word and as you do, ask God to open your eyes to these truths.

The Violin

Have you ever received news that has cut your heart to the core? Several years ago, I received phone calls, two nights in a row, from two different friends struggling in their marriage. My heart hurt for them, because their hearts were broken. I tried to encourage them to do whatever it took to work things out. I prayed with them and for them.

After the second call, I hung up the phone wondering what was going on. I know so many divorced people and many more who are struggling in their marriages. This trend has left so many children and family members hurt, broken and wondering what has happened to their world. As I write this short story, I want to be clear that this is geared towards men.

In Ephesians 5:25, we find a command to men, "Husbands, love your wives, just as Christ also loved the church and gave Himself for it."

Well, from scripture we know:

1. Christ died for the church.
2. That Christ sits at the right hand of the Father making intercession for us. In other words, "Christ lives for the church."
3. We are commanded to love our wives just as Christ loves the church.

Friend, I personally don't know a man who would not *die* for his wife. If necessary, every man I know would take a bullet to save his wife. He would put his life on the line to save her. But there is something else that I believe is a part of the problem why marriages are being destroyed.

Friend, the question is, "Will you *live* for your wife?" Let me explain; it's not every day our wives get to see us dying for them. Aren't you glad? However, our wives can, on a daily basis, see us live for them. How? Without your wife ever saying a word, do you pick your socks up off the floor for her? Do you put your dirty clothes away for her? Do you wash the dishes for her? Do you take time to think about something you could do that would bless her socks off?

Friend, why is it easy to say, "I will die for my wife," yet it seems so hard to live for her? Answer: Because we actually have to do something, to quit being selfish, to think outside the box. We did this when we dated.

After receiving the two phone calls, I began to think about this and how often I had failed in this area. So after a little thought, I went to a music store and rented a violin. Then I wrote a note that read "from your #1 fan." I placed the note in the case under the violin and gave it to my wife. No, no, I have not lost my mind, I found it! See, for a long time, my wife had been hinting she would like to learn to play the violin and I had missed it. I live and talk with her every day yet somehow I missed it.

Friend, does your wife know you are her #1 fan? Don't say, "I think so." Make sure she knows. We have got to stop assuming everything is okay in our relationship with our wives.

Think about it…When two people marry they become one, so to live for your wife is to actually live for yourself. Help yourself out today. Live for your wife.

The Toilet

Pride; it's an interesting thing. It shows the mentality of thinking it's 'all about me'. Pride desires all the attention, honor and glory. To some extent, we all struggle with pride. As Christian people, pride should have no part in our lives, but it is interesting how life in general sets us up to deal with pride on certain occasions.

My oldest son is normally a down-to-earth and humble young man but this story finds him on top of his world, then quickly snatched back to reality.

My wife homeschooled our two boys until they reached the ninth grade. As Mitchell, my oldest son, was finishing the eighth grade, we knew he was ready for public school. He was involved in sports and had many friends at church attending the local school so we decided this would be a good opportunity for him.

So starting with the ninth grade, Mitchell went from a school of two to a school of 1800+ students. It turns out this was the right move for us. Mitchell did very well in his studies and even made the JV baseball team. Even though Mitchell had played ball since he was six, making the baseball team at this school was no small accomplishment. This school, in its eleven-year history, has won five state titles, so Mitchell was excited just to have made the team.

Mitchell is tall lanky and left-handed. His position is pitcher and he had the privilege of pitching with six or seven really good pitchers who were on the team. In the tenth grade, he got the call to pitch against their county rival, Evans.

Mitchell was so excited but I knew he was under great pressure to win. And to win, he had to bring his best stuff forward because Evans always had very good talent and this year would be no different.

I would love to say Mitchell pitched a perfect game, but this would be prideful (ha-ha)...and it would not be the truth. Actually, Mitchell didn't throw badly and sure, they hit him but a solid defense kept the game close. Mitchell's pitch count was low so the coach let him pitch the entire game, down to the last out. All he needed was one out to win the game, but Mitchell had given his all. The coach put in a relief pitcher; he got the out and our team got the win!

We had to do some minor remodeling when he got home ... it seems his head would not fit through the door. Actually, when Mitchell got home, before we could celebrate with him and let him gloat, he had to use the restroom. We heard him call for us to come where he was. The toilet had stopped up and was beginning to overflow. I gave him the plunger and told him how to use it, then, being the dad I am, I ran to get my camera. I had to get a picture of this. I have the best picture of the winning pitcher, using that big left arm to plunge the toilet.

Isn't it amazing how quickly we can be humbled and brought back to reality? We read in Proverbs 6:16-17, "These six things the Lord hates, Yes, seven are an abomination to Him..." What is the first thing He lists? A prideful look! If you flip your bible pages over two chapters, God says, "...Pride and arrogance and the evil way and the perverse mouth I hate." (Proverbs 8:13)

Friend, the fact that you even woke up this morning and are breathing air into your lungs, is God's grace on your life. Yet for whatever reason or situation, we have pride; we try to steal the glory that belongs to God. How can we glory in anything but God, when the fact that we are even living is because of God?

Friend, there is nothing special about you or me. But there is something special about the God we serve. Today let's start giving God the glory for the great things He has done!

Never-Seez

I was plowing a field and noticed the points on the plow were worn and dull. The really cool thing about these points is, they are reversible. You just take the bolts out, spin the points 180 degrees and put the bolts back in. It sounds so easy but, to be honest, you don't just take the bolts out; they are a pain to get off. Years of rust from the dirt, rain and weather make this a chore.

I sought the help of my son, Justin. Using a lot of penetrating oil, a wire brush and every wrench, pliers and tool we had, we finally loosened each bolt. Once we spun the point around, we reattached either new bolts or the old bolts we had cleaned.

I had the bright idea of using Never-Seez on the bolts before reinstalling them. Never-Seez is a graphite lubricant that helps to prevent bolts and nuts from corroding. This enables them to be removed with relative ease at a later date. Never-Seez is thick and grayish in color. But the important thing to remember when using it is that a little goes a long way and if you are not careful, it will be all over you.

I handed Justin the can of Never-Seez, explained how to put it on the bolts and let him handle the rest. Every now and then, I would glance over at Justin and see how he was doing.

First, I noticed he had Never-Seez on his fingers. A while later, I glanced over and noticed it was slowly creeping up his hands. Before it was over, I had tears in my eyes from laughing so much. He had that stuff everywhere: on the back of his hands, his forearms, face and even on his nose. It was like some live thing from a horror movie, slowly taking over his body.

Then it hit me...In II Timothy 2:22, why does Paul challenge Timothy to flee youthful lust? Because it is like

Never-Seez; you start with opening the can and the next thing you know, it's all over you.

Friend, we who claim the name of Christ must stop playing with sin! Don't think for a moment that you have it under control. Don't think for a moment, "I will just open the can and take a look." You must throw the can down and run from it.

Friend, we cannot play with the things of the devil!!! If we give him an inch, he will take a mile. The next time you find yourself with Satan's can of Never-Seez, throw it down and run.

The Right Moment

My son who plays guitar wanted to buy a better quality guitar, so I checked with Wayne, a friend of mine who also plays. I asked him what brand or model he would suggest for my son. Wayne suggested a guitar, which was priced around $600. I told him my son didn't have that much money saved up, but he insisted it would be better to purchase a better quality guitar like this one.

Then Wayne said, "Let's check eBay." Now, I use computers every day at work, but I am really not the computer type and I don't have an eBay account, Facebook, My Space or any other type account. Wayne said, "Let me check; I would love to help your son find a guitar."

Wayne was on the hunt. Actually, in no time at all he had found the exact model guitar on eBay. The guitar appeared to be used very little and was in excellent shape. It even came with a very nice hard shell case. Go Wayne!!!

When Wayne told me about the guitar, he said the bid started at $250. I am thinking; I like it, but what will the ending price be? Wayne asked how much money Mitchell had saved up. When I told him, he said, "Good, I have a plan."

Wayne's plan was to wait until the last minute, in the last hour, on the last day of the bidding to make his move. Then a few seconds before the bidding was to stop, he would jump in with a bid. The plan sounded good to me. The last day came and the bid price had gotten to $360 with 45 seconds left to bid. Wayne waited until the last few seconds and placed a bid of $365.01 and Wayne won the bid! My son got his guitar for $365.01 and a few dollars shipping.

I thought about this and two things came to mind. First, it is a blessing to have friends who can help my children in ways I can't. Secondly, it reminded me of eternal life.

Friend, there are many people who play games when it comes to their eternal destiny. Too many people know they are not right with God. Yet they gamble with their lives, thinking that on the next to the last breath, they will get right with God. It is one thing to chance buying a guitar at a good price; but it's totally different to chance your eternal destination.

Friend, if you are not walking daily in a personal relationship with God, then you most likely don't know Him and His saving grace. Don't try to pretend or fool yourself; deep down in your heart you know where you really stand with God.

In I John 1:5-6, John makes it very clear, "This is the message we have heard from Him (Jesus) and declare to you, that God is light and in Him (God) there is no darkness at all. **IF** we say we have fellowship with Him (God), and walk in darkness, we **lie** and do not practice the truth."

Friend, at ten years old, I walked the aisle of the church and got baptized. Do you know what I really got? Wet! Because in the years following, I did not live for God. My desire was not to please Him, but myself. My life consisted of pain and hurt for others and myself. I knew about God but did not really know God.

However, at age 20, I was living and working in North Carolina. One night in my garage apartment, immersed in sin and all alone, God brought the reality of who I was to my mind. I had walked in darkness and practiced a lie. But, that night, God reached down in the mucky, miry pit of life and when His hand scraped the bottom, He brought me out and saved my soul.

Friend, my hope is built on nothing less than Jesus Christ and His righteousness! What is your hope built on?

The Bronze Star

I worked with Jesse for twelve years. He was much older than me and I was just twenty-one when I started working with him. He was actually older than my dad was and I remember he always wore suspenders. I knew Jesse was a godly man. I had many conversations with him about our faith and the God we worshipped. Jesse was quiet most of the time. He was soft-spoken with a great sense of humor and I loved to cut up with him. He used to tell me, "Boy, don't start no rooten and tooten, and there won't be no cuttin and shootin."

I remember when we worked twelve-hour night shifts and had only one night a week off. We worked together like this for about five weeks straight. To make it through those long hours, we would bring in all kinds of food to snack on. We had chips, dips, cookies, cakes, pies, ice cream and such. Every time we came back to the shop, we would snack on something.

After several weeks of this, Jesse must have thought he was gaining a few pounds. We have in our shop a set of scales, just like the black and white ones at the doctor's office; the kind of scales where you have to slide the big weight over, then slide the smaller weight across the bar until the bar floats. I happened to be standing about five feet from the scales when Jesse walked by and stepped up on them.

Another coworker saw me as I slipped up behind Jesse and put my foot on the back of the scale. Jesse kept sliding that weight over. When the bar finally floated, with Jesse's weight and the weight of my foot, he read the scale and slammed the small weight over in total disgust. I had jumped off and moved back to where I was originally standing. Jesse turned and stepped off the scale.

My coworker saw the whole thing and through his ear to ear grin, asked, "Jesse How much do you weigh?" Jesse stopped walking, putting both of his thumbs under the straps of his suspenders. Then he leaned back and as he ran his thumbs up his chest, pulling out on the suspenders said, "Heaviest I have ever been!"

I looked at my coworker and when our eyes met we burst into tears. I thought we would die laughing. Jesse never said a word but took it in stride, though I do believe he could have done some "cuttin and shootin" that day.

He eventually retired and ten years later, died. When we read his obituary, we learned something about him that we were not aware of. I knew he was a Christian man and I knew he had retired after twenty-two years in the military. But I didn't know that Jesse had served in the Korean War and the Vietnam War.

As we continued to read his obituary, it was full of military honors and medals. One of my coworkers noticed that Jesse had earned a Bronze Star with 2 oak-leaf clusters. Not being familiar with the military, I had no clue what this meant. My coworker informed me the military doesn't just give out bronze stars. How did we miss it? All those years of working with Jesse and we had no idea. If only I had spent time asking about his military service. How many stories died that day that will never be told?

In Hosea 4:4 and 6, we find a harsh judgment, "Hear the word of the Lord, You children of Israel, for the Lord brings a charge against the inhabitants of the land: There is no truth or mercy or knowledge of God in the land." Verse 6 goes on to say, "My people are destroyed for lack of knowledge."

Friend, God wants us to know Him. He wants us to ask questions, to learn of Him and to seek and find. He has given us His word to do this. Yet so often we are involved with church things but lack knowledge of Him. Don't treat God like I treated my friend, Jesse. Get to know Him, spend time in His word and ask questions.

The Cornfield

America is a beautiful country. To say I am an American traveler would be well overstated. However, I have been to several states and the beauty of America runs deep. I prefer to travel on two-lane roads and through the countryside. I enjoy the farms, the small quaint towns and the places people don't tend to think or talk about.

Each year for Christmas, my parents started giving us three boys a week at the beach. So we really don't get our Christmas until May. This is such a wonderful idea, because it gets the whole family together. Besides, Mom and Dad love having all nine grandchildren together.

Back in May of 2006, we were on our Christmas vacation traveling through Georgia to a beach just below Tallahassee, Florida. As we traveled, we passed farms of onions, wheat, beans, cotton, pecan orchards and such. But, the one field that caught my eye was a cornfield. This corn was amazingly already beautiful and very tall, yet it had been a somewhat dry spring. The field was planted in a circle and was watered by a pivot irrigation system.

My mind began to wander back to being a kid and flipping through my dad's Progressive Farmer magazines. I remember seeing arial photos of pivot irrigation fields and thought how cool they looked.

So anyway, I am driving along checking out this cornfield and noticed a few things. The corn under the irrigation system was about seven or eight feet tall, yet the corn at the edge of the sprinkler tapered off to about three to four feet tall. I also noticed the tall corn was a lush green color and the smaller corn was a brownish, yellowish color. In fact, the smaller corn looked stunted and stressed.

I thought about my own life and how this picture of the corn applied to me. I wish I could say I lived my entire

49

Christian life under the refreshing rain of the Holy Spirit, but this is just not the case. All too often I found myself on the outskirts, out on the edge. I found myself being stunted and stressed, lacking the vibrant green lushness of new growth.

Friend, I have come to learn that too many of us are like this. We want the name "corn." We like being called "corn" because when it's harvest time, we want to be picked. But in the meantime, we would rather live our lives on the outside edge doing as we please. Thinking we are doing well when in actuality, we are stunted, stressed and unproductive.

As we read in Hebrews 5:12-14, think about these words and your own life, "For by this time you ought to be teachers, you need someone to teach you again the first principles of the oracles of God; and you have come to need milk and not solid food. For everyone who partakes only of milk is unskilled in the word of righteousness, for he is a babe. But solid food belongs to those who are of full age, that is, those who by reason of use have their senses exercised to discern both good and evil."

Friend, it is not funny the least bit to see a grown, capable man drinking milk from a bottle and eating baby food; and yet so many Christians are doing just that! We are all guilty of this at times, but it is time to throw down the bottle and pick up a fork and knife.

Friend, here is the difference between us and the corn... The corn has no option; it's planted where it's planted. But we have an option to move. We can begin to draw near the center pivot and be refreshed, renewed and productive.

Friend, let's throw down the bottle and pick up the fork and knife; let's move on and start cutting into the solid food of God's word.

The Drug Test

As a rule, many businesses require random drug testing and it is common in the place where I am employed. So I was not surprised when I was told to appear for a drug test. You know the routine. I gave a urine sample to the company nurse. After doing the required test, she said, "You have blood in your urine. You need to see a doctor."

I didn't feel like I had blood in my urine. In fact, I didn't feel sick at all; I felt perfectly fine. Thank you!!!

I am a man and being the typical man I am, I did what typical men do...nothing! And to prove I am a typical man, I surely did not tell my wife. Well... two weeks later, I was out on the front porch. I was not out there visiting a neighbor, or checking the weather, nor was I out there to sit in the rocking chair. I was out there hanging over the handrail in horrible pain and puking my head off, and in the most horrible pain I have ever experienced. People, I am at the gate of death. I believe my fingerprints are still in the wood on the front rail.

My lovely wife doesn't have a clue what is going on with me... neither did I. I was sweating like I was in the desert and white as a ghost so she called my mom. She asked Mom to hurry so we could get to the emergency room.

When mom arrived, I was sitting in a chair watching television and feeling perfectly fine. I told my wife I didn't need to go to the emergency room. (I told you I am a typical man.)

Mom interrupts, "I know what it is." Oh no! I am outnumbered. Mom says, "You have a kidney stone." (By the way, mom is not a doctor, but she did stay in a Holiday Inn Express at some point in her life.) Then she continued, "I have seen your dad go through the same thing before. Thanks, Dad.

Anyway, I just wanted to go to bed, but I was fighting a losing battle. Next thing I know, I am in the emergency

51

room having to put on this gown, with the slit in the front or back, depending on which way you put it on. I was thinking, "Give me two gowns. I will put them both on and we don't have to worry about a slit."

By the way, what kind of "weirdo" came up with one little string trying to hold the entire gown closed? Get real, people; even my jacket has more than one button holding it together. I just wanted to be home and if I thought it would work, I would have clicked my heels together like Dorothy did in The Wizard of Oz.

The emergency room doctor came in and my wife tells him everything. She even told him about my family history…"The stone family." By this time, it was about midnight and I felt like I have been stoned.

They x-rayed my lower back and kidneys. Sure enough, I had a whopper of a stone. By this time, I 'fessed' up and told them about the drug test and what the company nurse said about having blood in my urine and needing to see a doctor. I cut my eyes over toward my wife. Her mouth was wide open like a flycatcher and she gave me "the look."

Friend, I knew something was happening. I had the signs, but I chose to ignore them. I must have thought, "If I ignore it, it will go away." The bible gives us signs about the end times. We can ignore them, but in reality it's coming. Check out these passages:

- II Timothy 3:1-5, "But know this, that in the last days perilous times will come: For men will be lovers of themselves, lovers of money, boasters, proud, blasphemers, disobedient to parents, unthankful, unholy, unloving, unforgiving, slanderers, without self-control, brutal, despisers of good, traitors, headstrong, haughty, lovers of pleasure rather than lovers of God, having a form of godliness but denying it's power."
- We also find some signs from the Sermon on the Mount in Matthew 24. Jesus gives us many indications of His return yet don't miss verse 36, "But of the day

52

and hour no one knows, not even the angels of heaven, but my Father only."

Friend, I had the signs, I knew something was going to happen. But I had no idea what day or hour. Friend, Jesus is coming back; you have the signs even though you don't know the time.

Are You Excited? Are You Ready?

Preacher

The company I work for hired several new employees into our shop. I happened to be working with one of the new guys when Roy, a fellow coworker, passed by. Roy stopped and asked my new coworker a question. Has Phil preached to you yet? My new coworker had a funny look on his face, while I felt a big grin coming over mine.

It's normal when working with new people to tell them about yourself or ask them about their lives. You know the routine. "Where did you work before?" "How long were you there?" "Are you married?" "How long?" "Have any children?" "Boy or girl?" "What are their ages?" "What are your hobbies?" Normally, the conversation ends up with you or them talking about something you really enjoy. It doesn't really take but a few hours of conversation to find out what makes people tick.

But all day long, rolling around in the back of my mind, (and believe me, I have plenty of empty room for things to roll around in my mind), were the words that Roy said, "Has Phil preached to you yet?"

What if Roy could have said things like, "Has Phil told you about the porno tapes he has?" or "Has Phil told you about the wild parties he throws?" or "Has Phil told you about the girlfriend he has on the side that his wife doesn't know about?" I thought, what an honor to be known as a preacher. But you know what? *We are all preachers*!!! *W*hat separates us is the <u>subject</u> of our preaching.

Friend, if a Roy had walked by you, what would he have said about you? What do you preach each day? You know, by the words you say and the life you live, what do you preach?

Romans 10:9-15 says, "That if you confess with your mouth the Lord Jesus and believe in your heart that God had raised Him from the dead, you will be saved. For with the heart one believes to righteousness and with the mouth confession is made to salvation." For the scripture says, "Whoever believes on Him will not be put to shame. For there is no distinction between Jew and Greek, for the same Lord over all is rich to all who call upon Him. For whoever calls upon the name of the Lord shall be saved." (Friend, do not miss these last verses.) "How then shall they call on Him in whom they have not believed? And how shall they believe in Him of whom they have not heard? *And how shall they hear without a preacher?* And how shall they preach unless they are sent?"

Friend, you may not be the best speaker; I am surely not! You may not have all the answers; I surely don't! But let me ask you a question. Can you proclaim what Christ has done in your life? Or better yet, will you proclaim what Christ has done in your life? God has placed you exactly where you are and you are preaching something. What are they hearing?

Will I Be A Kid In Heaven

Justin, my youngest son, was such a neat kid. He was the kind of kid you could put in a sandbox and he would entertain himself for days. Using sticks, leaves and such from the yard, he would build the most awesome bridges, tunnels and roads. Hour after hour, he would push his little cars, trains and trucks over the intertwined highways he had built.

Justin loved to play. I remember one time we were down at the pond playing in the water. Jacob, his best friend, was there and they got into some mud. Next thing I know, they spread the mud all over themselves. They were covered from their heads to their toes. I did what every other dad would do; I ran for the camera. What great pictures, what great memories!

Justin also loved to build things with the blocks and toys in his room. I loved to go in my boys' room with the video camera and interview them. I would ask them questions to see what was on their minds. This was especially difficult with Justin because he really didn't talk much.

But I will never forget one particular question my little boy asked me and I wished I'd had my video camera then. We were in his room and he was playing, when out of the blue he asked, "Dad, will I be a kid in heaven?" Sometimes our children stump us and leave us speechless. I finally muttered out the words, "I don't know! Why do you ask?" Justin paused and replied "Because I love being a kid." Oh my goodness! Did you catch that? Justin loves who he is!!!

Friend, we live in a society where people struggle with who they are. They don't like the way they look, so they spend billions of dollars each year trying to change themselves with clothes, makeup, plastic surgery, exercise equipment, dieting plans, hair products, etc. Notice I am not saying people should not try to look nice and be healthy. Keep reading and you will get my point. The problem is people feel like they never measure up to a certain worldly standard and as a result, they never get to enjoy being who God made them. I believe this is one of Satan's greatest tools to distract people.

In Matthew 22:37-39, we find a wonderful command that will set our thinking straight; "You shall love the Lord your God with all your heart, with all your soul, and with all your mind. This is the first and great commandment. The second is like it: You shall love your neighbor as yourself."

Friend, I believe people have no problem loving themselves. People naturally desire to place themselves first, above all else. People are self-protecting, self-preserving, self-loving and down right selfish. But I really don't believe people love who they are.

When people begin to love God like verse 37 says and they begin to understand who God is and have that wonderful relationship with Him, the byproduct will be that they love who they are. And when a person loves God and loves being a child of God, loving our neighbor becomes second nature.

Friend, do you know who you are? Do you love who you are? It all starts with a loving God, who first loved us enough not to ignore our sins.

The Spike

Back in the early 90's my dad was invited to go pheasant hunting with his brother and a local friend who had been pheasant hunting since 1980. A group of local friends including my dad and uncle were off to Kansas for a week of hunting. Bear in mind, it is a nineteen-hour hour drive from Georgia to Kansas, so pheasant hunting must be a tremendous amount of fun.

In the late 1990's, one of the regular guys couldn't go on the trip, so I was invited. Having never pheasant hunted before, I had no clue what to expect but I knew nineteen hours in a truck was a very long trip.

Driving across the American heartlands was beautiful. I even got to visit the Arch in St. Louis, the "Gateway to the West."

Here I am traveling where countless others have gone before. The difference was that I was in a climate controlled, comfortable truck and they were in horse-drawn wagons, but that is just one difference. These people were searching for a new life, a new start, a new fortune and new opportunities. These people were to face hardships, dangers and losses you and I have never known.

Anyway, we finally got to Kansas and while it was not the end of the world, you could see it from there. We were in the middle of nowhere and I found myself loving it. Nothing but farms, farms and more farms with little farming towns scattered every umpteen miles. It made me want to strap on a six-shooter and ride a horse; until I stepped outside and the freezing wind was blowing thirty miles an hour.

Think I will just ride in the truck for now...and by the way, turn up the heater, please. No wonder the wind is blowing like crazy...somebody cut down all the trees. Haven't these people heard of reforestation?

Several farmers were extremely generous to us and allowed us to hunt on their land. Field after field planted in wheat, soybeans, corn and milo, which is a grain. All the fields were laid out in perfect rows.

So I now find myself in Kansas, where the land is open, the sky seems so vast and fields seem to go on for days. But…pheasant hunting is work! I am thinking that instead of walking a million miles a day flushing up birds, we need dogs trained to run the birds to us while we sit in place. But friend, I will never get over the excitement of that first pheasant getting up at my feet.

Pheasants are about the size of a small chicken; the males have long tails and multi-colored feathers that are absolutely beautiful, especially when the sun shines on them. To describe the cackle the pheasant makes when it is flushed up is difficult, but let's just say it will get your blood pumping fast on a cold winter day. Pheasant hunting is a wonderful experience, but hunting with my dad is what I really enjoyed. This was priceless.

Once, while hunting, we crossed an old railroad bed. As I walked, my eye caught a glimpse of something on the ground. The tracks of the railroad had long been removed but as I kicked around with my foot, I found an old railroad spike. As I reached down and picked up that cold, metal spike, I wondered… "How old must this be; how many people must have handled this spike; who was the person who nailed it in the timber to hold the rail down?"

Then I thought of the spikes the Roman soldiers used on Jesus and wondered what they were like? Somehow, I couldn't throw that worthless spike down, so I dropped it into my pocket. All day long, as I carried that spike, I thought about the cross and the spikes that held Jesus to the cross.

Spikes that held Jesus to the cross? STOP!!! Hold on there. It finally hit me. How could I have been so slow to think? Could a spike hold the God of the Bible, my God, to a cross? Could an iron spike hold Jesus on the cross?

In John 18, Judas betrayed Jesus with a kiss. There is a whole mob and an attachment of Roman troops who had come to take Jesus away. When they arrived, Jesus asked, "Whom are you seeking?" then they answered, "Jesus of Nazareth!"

Friend, don't miss the power of God, which John will describe in the next verse when He said to them, "I am He." They drew back and fell to the ground. The power of Jesus' words is such that the whole mob and troops who came to take him away, found themselves utterly helpless and piled up on the ground. Think about it, even the spoken words of Jesus were like a giant bowling ball that had knocked them over like pins, tumbling to the ground. A perfect strike at that.

In the book of Matthew, chapter 26, we find the same story. Don't miss what Matthew notes in his documentation of this event. I will pick up in verse 51, "And suddenly one of those who were with Jesus stretched out his hand and drew his sword, struck the servant of the high priest, and cut off his ear. Then Jesus said to him, Put your sword in its place, for all who take the sword will perish by the sword. Or do you not think that I cannot now pray to my Father, and He will provide Me with more than twelve legions of angels?"

Not that Jesus would need twelve legions of angels, but He is teaching his disciples and us that He is in perfect control. Think about it friend; No mob could have just walked in the garden and taken Jesus unless He let them. And no spike could have held Him to that cross unless He let it!

Friend, yes there were spikes nailed through His hands and feet, but it wasn't the spikes; it was His wonderful love for us that held Him to the cross!

Remember the words of the old Hymn:

"He could have called ten thousand angels to destroy the world and set Him free, but He died alone for you and me!"

Friend, do you know this love of God? If so, how has knowing this love changed you?

A Golfer's Dream

Several years ago, my oldest son, Mitchell and I were driving in town. We were traveling down Washington Road. To our left, we passed many restaurants and a few shopping centers. To our right was a wall. The wall is a combination of green shrubs, hedges, foliage, trees and a fence somewhere in the middle of it all. The wall of foliage was so dense you could not see through it. As we are traveling past, Mitchell said, "Behind those trees is a golfer's dream."

Now, this may seem like a very odd statement, but let me explain. We live about 30 minutes from Augusta, Georgia. Need I say more??? Anyway, Augusta is home to the "Augusta National," which was built by the great golfer, Bobby Jones. The National is perhaps the most prestigious golf course in the world. Each spring, when the dogwood trees and azaleas are in full bloom, you will find the greatest golfers in the world playing the "Masters Tournament" on this course.

I am not a golfer, but I have been very fortunate a few times to get tickets to the tournament. I will admit, the grounds are absolutely breathtaking. And, as for playing on the course... well you will have to ask the likes of Jack Nicklaus, Arnold Palmer, Phil Mickelson, and Tiger Woods to name a few.

Mitchell's words, "Behind those trees is a golfer's dream," kept coming to my mind. Think about how many people must pass by the National each day; the most prestigious golf course in the world and yet most of these people never give it a second thought. That night, I happened to be reading Matthew 25 when Mitchell's words came back to me but in a different light. In Matthew 24 and 25, the passage known as the Olivet Discourse, Jesus speaks about judgment and the last days.

In Matthew 25:31-46, we find God's judgment. God will separate the "sheep" (His children) on the right, from the "goats" (those without the saving knowledge of Christ) who will be on the left. The main difference between the sheep and goats will be their focus. The sheep, out of their love for Jesus focus on others. But, the goats have their focus on themselves. At the judgment, the sheep will be blessed with the presence of God, living in His kingdom. God calls the goats cursed and they will be in everlasting fire, prepared for the devil and his angels. And Jesus goes on to explain that their heart was never for Him.

In Matthew 25:42-43, Jesus says, "For I was hungry and you gave Me no food; I was thirsty and you gave Me no drink; I was a stranger and you did not take Me in; naked and you did not clothe Me; sick and in prison and you did not visit Me." Then those who are judged as goats will try to act ignorant and ask, "When did we see you this way?" In verse 45, we find Jesus' reply, "Then He will answer them saying, Assuredly I say to you, inasmuch as you did not do it to one of the least of these, you did not do it to Me."

Friend, people pass by the world's most famous golf course and never give it a second thought. They have become so caught up in their own daily pursuits, they don't even think about what is around them. I believe we do the same thing with God. At first, we might see the needs around us. But, soon we become calloused and before you know it, our eyes are open but we don't see.

Friend, unless we daily keep fresh in our hearts the saving grace of God and the love of God poured out in our lives, we will continue to ride through life with our eyes open, yet not seeing.

Friend, pray that God will slow you down enough and open your eyes to see what he sees today. Remember, when you do it to the least of these…you do it unto Him.

A Brother's Wisdom

We were on vacation and I was fishing with my older brother, John. We were talking about how our children were getting older. You know, the age where they get into all kinds of activities like football, karate, baseball, basketball, soccer, swimming...you get the picture. Everyone is running in different directions every night of the week. As I began to tell John about the busyness of my life, he interrupted and told me a mind-pricking statement. You know, one of those statements that stops you in your tracks and one you will never forget.

John said to me, "Phillip, you will always be busy. Make sure you are busy doing the right thing!" How true this is!!! We are all busy doing some things or many things, but are we doing the right things?

There is a passage in Luke 10:38-42 that describes our busy lives to a T. Not only that; this passage gives us an example of what our priorities should be. "Now it happened as they went that Jesus entered a certain village; and a certain woman named Martha welcomed Him into her house. And she had a sister called Mary, who also sat at Jesus feet and heard His word. But Martha was distracted with much serving and she approached Him and said, Lord, do You not care that my sister has left me to serve alone? Therefore tell her to help me. And Jesus answered and said to her, Martha, Martha you are worried and troubled about many things. But one thing is needed and Mary has chosen that good part, which will not be taken away from her."

Friend, Martha was the one who invited Jesus over, and yet she had no time for Him. She was busy preparing a wonderful meal, making sure everyone was comfortable and that they had plenty to drink. Was she doing bad things? Absolutely not! All the things she was doing were good things.

But something was missing and all these things began to weigh her down. She began to point her finger. Her mind began to be confused and she thought her whole problem was that Mary was doing nothing. "That's it, that do-nothing Mary is my problem," she must have thought.

One of Martha's problems was that she could not see. She was blinded to the fact that Mary was very busy. Mary was very busy doing the right thing at the right time. What was she doing, you ask? She was busy listening and learning at the feet of her Savior. Did you notice what was not said or implied? The Scriptures said nothing of Mary being agitated, frustrated, or being burned out.

Friend, as my brother John said, "You will always be busy..." The question is, are you busy doing the right thing?

I am far from being the most effective with my time, but I learned to practice this...that I couldn't add without subtracting. So before Terri and I add something to our family schedule, whether it has to do with the boys, or us we must figure out what to subtract out. The problem is that if we don't do this, like Martha, the first thing to go is our time with God. Then we end up being agitated, frustrated or just burned out.

The #1 Game In America

What is the #1 game in America? 'Baseball, it's got to be baseball, America's game, right?' Still others would argue, 'It's football. Football has to be America's game.' Then you would have those who will argue, 'America's #1 game is basketball.' With Beckham coming to America, some are trying to make soccer the #1 game in America. What Do I say? I believe the # 1 game in America is the "blame game."

Let me give you an example, while the term "blame game" sinks into your mind. When my boys were younger, they were involved in a mission organization at church called Royal Ambassadors. They were taught about missions, missionaries and how to be involved in missions. But they would also do other fun things like camping out. The boys and their dads would go camping and we would try (notice I said try), to incorporate the teaching of missions while on our camping trip.

I remember one campout when we had a great big blazing campfire with about twenty-five young boys running around playing while we dads were conversing. And as you know how boys are, at least one-third of them were pyromaniacs. So, we adults are having to constantly tell them, "Don't poke in the fire; don't run through the woods with that stick on fire; and stop shoving each other while standing near the fire."

Finally having had "enough," another dad and I got a shovel and dug out a bunch of coals and made a path about 3 foot wide and 20 feet long. Then we got all the pyromaniacs to take their shoes off and made them fire-walk through the coals barefooted. We thought this would calm down their wanting to play in the fire. (Actually, we did not do this; it isn't true. I just thought I would give you a little shock in the story. Not that it didn't cross our minds...)

67

Anyway, all these little pyromaniacs were running around the fire and we dads were just talking, when all of a sudden we heard this extremely loud explosion. It was like a small bomb exploding and suddenly, the sky above the fire was filled with red glowing sparks. People jumped like there was no tomorrow. What in the world was going on? It seems several of the boys were daring each other and somehow an unopened can of coke was thrown into the fire. {Caution! Warning! Danger! Let me warn you now. Children, <u>do not</u> try this at home. This stunt is very dangerous and was performed by a seven-year-old stunt boy.} Or, at least he thought he was. Who knows what goes through the mind of a seven-year-old?

Anyway, back to the story. You will never guess what game was played next. I will give you a hint. It was not basketball or soccer. You are 100% right. It was the "blame game," America's #1 game. All these little boys pointing fingers and it wasn't at themselves.

When and where did America's #1 game start? In Genesis, chapter 3, we find Adam and Eve. They had both just sinned and been found out when we get the first glimpse of the "blame game." Let's pick up reading in verses 12- 13:

- Verse 12, "Then the man said, "The woman whom You gave to be with me, she gave me of the tree, and I ate."
- Verse 13, And the Lord God said to the woman, "What is this you have done?" And the woman said, "The serpent deceived me, and I ate."

So, in verse 12, we find Adam blaming God and Eve. While in verse 13, we see Eve blaming the serpent. The # 1 game in America and the world started in the Garden of Eden. And it continues to be the most popular game to this day.

Friend, are you playing this game? If so, stop! Stop blaming others and God for your own disobedience to His Word and plan for your life. The fact is that many Christians are paralyzed in their Christian growth, marriages, families, jobs and relationships because they refuse to stop playing the "blame game." As popular as it is and you know it is; the "blame game" is a terrible game to play!

The River

One of the toughest things as a parent is to get your children out of the house to try new things. I am not the best at it but I do try to get my children involved in different things. One particular time, I borrowed a couple of kayaks from a friend. I thought it would be great to take my son, Justin, on the Savannah River near our home.

It was a cold winter day in February, but a beautiful afternoon. We drove to the river just below the dam and unloaded the gear. I made sure we had on enough warm clothes and strapped on our lifejackets. As we climbed into the kayaks and pushed off onto the river, I was surprised at how full it was from the winter rain.

The river was pleasantly calm and peaceful. Justin and I paddled up the river a few hundred yards to the dam and then turned our kayaks downstream. As we began to paddle and drift downstream, our eyes shifted from the massive concrete dam to the beautiful river that lay below it.

Do you ever have those crazy thoughts like, 'I hope this dam doesn't burst. If it does, we will have one heck of a ride'. But I wasn't about to disturb Justin's peaceful kayak ride with my crazy thoughts, or at least not until we were safely back at the truck.

Anyway, we are enjoying the relaxing calmness of the river, when we saw a few groups of ducks fly over. When you are enjoying what you are doing, time slips by quickly and it did that day.

Justin was the one who said, "Dad, should we turn back?" I looked at my watch and saw it was 5:27 and thought he was right, because it would be getting dark soon.

As we turned around for the nice paddle back up to the boat landing, we had not gone too far when we heard this terribly loud horn blowing. I thought, "OH NO!" That horn meant they were about to generate electricity.

Soon the calmness of the river gave way to turbulent currents and our little casual paddle back upstream became a struggle.

I yelled to Justin, "Don't stop paddling!" If we had stopped paddling, the kayak would immediately begin to drift backwards. We had totally lost sight of the beauty, as we battled our way back upstream. I noticed Justin was struggling and tiring so I paddled my kayak over to the bank and wedged it against an overhanging tree.

As I waited for Justin to catch up, I noticed a fishing line tied to a limb on a tree just in front of me. The line looked to be new, fairly stout and about nine to ten feet long. My mind began to race. I paddled up to the line and removed it from the limb. I tied the ends together and twisted the fishing line to make four or five loops, a perfect towrope, I thought.

I looked back and noticed that Justin was exhausted and struggling to hold on to the tree. Taking the fishing line, I looped it around the tee handle on the back of my kayak and the tee handle on the front of his kayak. My last instruction to Justin before we pushed off into the turbulent river was to not stop paddling. As I pushed us off, I could hear the sound of his paddle cut through the cold swift water. We were paddling with all we had.

After about 100 to 125 yards, I noticed the river wasn't as turbulent as it had been. In fact, I noticed the speed of my kayak had accelerated a bit. It was then I looked back and noticed the homemade towrope had become disconnected.

As we made our way back to the landing in our sweat-soaked clothes, exhausted and out of breath, I looked at Justin and managed to speak these words. "Son, I will never view you as a little boy again. Little boys quit but young men don't! From now on you will be my young man because you did not quit."

As a side note, here is a great lesson... When things get tough, don't quit. How many marriages, jobs, opportunities and relationships are lost because we have unintentionally taught a generation it is okay to cut and run when life gets tough?

As we loaded the kayaks back in the truck with the sun sinking low in the sky, several things came to mind:

1. When you least expect it, life gets tough. (turbulent water)
2. When life gets tough, you must press on. To stop is to drift backwards ending in a worse condition.(paddling for all you are worth)
3. As you move forward in life, God will provide exactly what you need. (the fishing line)
4. As soon as God knows you are ready, He takes away what He provided.(the kayaks become disconnected)
5. No matter how difficult the situation is, you can always help someone else through their difficulty. (stopping to help Justin)

Friend, as you read the wonderful story of the Jewish people being led out of Egypt, you find over and over these truths in God's Word. The situation would get difficult and God would step in, providing what they needed at the time. Then, at the right time, He would take it away. Take time to read just one chapter, Exodus 16, and you will get a glimpse of what I am describing. Friend, will you live these truths in your own life? In your own life struggle, will you reach out to help bring someone else along?

XR75

When I was about ten years old, all I wanted was a motorcycle. I wanted a dirt bike and not just any dirt bike. My cousin, who was a year older than me, raced a Honda XR75. My best friend and his brother had motorcycles and I wanted a XR75 to the point I think I constantly dreamed about it.

I remember having a motorcycle magazine and inside was a Honda advertisement. After all those years, I still remember what it looked like. The ad featured a family; Dad, Mom, Sister and a boy about my age. They were standing or sitting on their bikes. The boy was with his new XR75 and he wore a red, white and blue jersey. I can't remember if he had a grin from ear to ear, but if he didn't, someone should have kicked him for not being thankful. I used to dream of being in that picture.

Christmas was coming soon and I knew what my present would be. Now, I knew Dad and Mom could not afford to purchase my two older brothers motorcycles, but it would be a different Christmas for me. The anticipation of that Christmas was almost more than this ten-year-old could bear. I dreamed of riding my new XR75 on Christmas Day. I wondered if Mom would let me bring it in the house so that I could sleep with it beside my bed. Of course, I would have to clean the mud off the tires first.

It was Christmas Eve. Excitement filled the air at the Knox's house, or at least around me. I knew better than to look for the XR75 by the tree so I had a plan. I would look for a box about the size of a helmet. It would be neatly wrapped sitting under the tree labeled "To Phillip, From Santa."

Finally Christmas morning came; I thought it would never get here. Bursting into the living room with my family, my eyes were surveying the presents. Mom and Dad always seemed to give our best present last. As the presents were given out, I didn't notice one shaped like a helmet box. I remember my last present was long, thin and rectangular shaped. I thought there must be a note in this present leading out to my new XR75. When I tore opened the present and opened the box, I got a shirt; a shirt with "Honda" written across the chest. There was no note and there were no more presents.

Anger filled my heart and my joy was gone. How could they? I only remember wearing the shirt a few times and then it was thrown in the back of my closet.

Years passed. I was married and had my own children and had long forgotten about that Christmas and the "Honda" shirt, when I got a phone call from my Mom. She was cleaning up and throwing things out and wanted me to come by and see if I wanted anything.

As I sorted through the items, my eyes became fixed on that "Honda" shirt. In an instant, all those memories flooded my mind. But I noticed something I had failed to notice as a ten-year-old boy. It wasn't just a "Honda" shirt. It was the same red, white, and blue jersey that the kid in the ad was wearing. My eyes filled with tears and my heart was sorrowful, as I understood that my parents had gone to the Honda dealer and bought me the best present they could afford.

This Christmas present is one of my most prized possessions. Even to this day, I keep my "Honda" jersey in my shirt drawer on the left-hand side as a reminder. Someone should have <u>kicked me</u> for not being thankful.

Friend, don't miss this. One of the greatest gifts I have ever received, I wasted. I threw it in the back of my closet and never received the maximum benefit from it. This is exactly what so many people do with God's greatest gift; His Son, Jesus. How many times, knowing you are a sinner and hearing the truths of His saving grace, have you thrown Jesus in the back of the closet? For whatever reason, God's greatest gift means nothing to you.

Friend, do not harden your heart today. It's not too late. I wasted years and even though I may not be able to wear the jersey now, I receive great enjoyment from it. And even though you have wasted many years and created much pain in your life, God's salvation is still available. Stop playing with God, for He is not playing with you.

Friend, do your eyes tear up with sorrow and your heart with repentance when you think of your sin and your neglect of Jesus? If so, there is good news for you! II Corinthians 6:1-2 states, "We then as workers together with Him also plead with you not to receive the grace of God in vain. For He says: In an acceptable time I have heard you, and in the day of salvation I have helped you. Behold, now is the accepted time; Behold, now is the day of salvation."

Friend, if this is your day, repent and believe. Today is the day and if you believe… don't do it in vain. For there is no throwing Jesus in the back of the closet for those who know His saving grace. You either 'wear Him or you don't!!!'

The Bayou Meto

I got a call from a duck-hunting friend of mine and he asked, "Where are you going to hunt ducks next weekend?" My duck season had not been too hot and he knew it. So when I paused in my response, he piped in saying, "Let's go to Arkansas."

He began to describe the place we were to hunt. The Bayou Meto is about fifteen to twenty thousand acres of flooded timber (hardwoods). I had only read about this type of hunting where you drive a small boat through channels to access the flooded timber where ducks liked to hang out.

This sounded like an adventure to me, so off we went to Arkansas; my friend, Ed, Mitchell, who is my oldest son and me. Even though it was late January, the weather was mild and a drive across our country is always beautiful, so how could we go wrong?

Once we arrived, we got our stuff unpacked where we were to stay. Then we loaded the boat and truck. When we had gotten to the ranger station and checked in, we launched our boat. The thrill and excitement of setting out into these vast flooded woods was an awesome feeling. Not realizing exactly how and where to hunt these vast flooded woods, we just parked our boat and tied it up to a tree on the edge of one of the channels.

To prevent getting lost and to be sure we would be able to find our boat when it was dark, we marked our boat with a GPS. Then off through the flooded timber we wandered looking for small openings in the timber where the ducks might fly in and we looked for any signs of ducks, like feathers and such. Using our GPS, we would mark these spots to hunt the next day.

The next morning, under complete darkness other than a head lamp and a small spotlight, we launched out again.

This cold winter morning brought a new sense of adventure and excitement as Ed maneuvered the boat through the narrow channels. Mitchell and I had never experienced this type of duck hunting before, but you can bet, we are loving it! I can already picture the ducks dropping through the timber right on our noses.

We were wearing waders to keep from getting wet, so with decoys on our backs, guns in our hands and our head lamps, we left our boat and headed out following our GPS to the place we had found to hunt the day before. We could hear other hunters driving their boats up and down the channel to their favorite hunting spots.

Suddenly, we heard a boat stop and turn into the woods right where we were. It began to travel through the woods directly towards us. In fact, the bright spotlights mounted to their boat blinded us. We shined our dimly lit head lights towards the boat but they didn't seem to notice. Actually, they drove ahead of us and were beating us to our hunting spot.

Then we noticed that our GPS pointed in the opposite direction of the boat that we thought was moving closer to our hunting spot. The boat disappears into the timber and darkness engulfs us once again, saved only by our dimly lit head lamps.

Here we are, wading through knee-deep water while we searched for our hunting spot thinking our GPS was broken. Totally frustrated, we talked about it and decided to travel only a few hundred yards further and hunt wherever we ended up.

We tossed out the decoys and stood in the knee-deep water surrounded by the cold dark woods. As dawn came, and boy was I glad when it did, I wish I could say we were in a wonderful spot full of ducks. However, we did see many ducks but not many were coming to where we were.

As morning wore on, we decided to cash in, so we picked up the decoys. I looked at my GPS and we decided to follow it. Only about 150 yards away was our duck hole. The boat that had passed by us was not going to our duck hole and our GPS was not broken. We were standing in the exact spot where we were the day before. Man, what a long, long disappointing walk back to the boat.

Riding back to the boat ramp with the cold crisp air biting our faces, my mind began to run through the events of the morning and the decisions we had made. If only...If only the boat had not cut us off, we would not have been distracted. If only...If only we had trusted our GPS. It had never let us down before. Why did we doubt it?

In Psalm 119, verse 105, we find these words, "Your word is a lamp unto my feet And a light to my path."

Friend, so often we fail simply because we fail to trust God's word. God's word has never failed you. It cannot fail you. It will not fail you. Yet, when certain things cross our path and our situation changes, we doubt. This should not be so.

Friend, take time to think of things that have or might cross your path and cause you to doubt the truth of God's Word. Then ask God to help you remain true to His Word when these times come. God will not fail you. God's word will not fail you. But we can fail ourselves.

Granny Jean Is Coming

Justin, my youngest son, loves his Granny Jean, my mother-in-law. Granny Jean lives about an hour and a half from us. Each time Granny Jean visits, it is the same routine. She would bring hugs and kisses, and I would go hide somewhere (I am just kidding. I have a wonderful mother-in-law). Then she had a bag full of all our favorites; some kind of treat; candy and books were Justin's favorites. He loved to snack on his favorite candy while sitting in Granny Jean's lap and listening to book after book being read. I know this was a favorite time for her as well.

We had informed our boys that Granny would be coming the next Saturday and they were looking forward to her coming, but Justin was really excited. That Saturday morning came and very early we heard Justin stirring around in his room. This was not too unusual for he was an early bird and we were used to him getting up early. Finally, we heard the front door open and slam shut.

I am thinking, "I am glad he is going to get the paper." It was nearing winter and there was a nice chill in the air waiting to sting my face a bit if I had to get the paper. Being the wonderful dad I am, I just lay in bed, waiting for the paper to arrive. Now before you jump to any conclusions about me, let me continue. Someone has to be the dad and I know it's a hard life but I am willing to sacrifice.

So, here I am lying in bed but no paper has arrived. What in the world is taking him so long? Well, to be honest, around 9:00 at night my mind and body systems start shutting down and by 9:30, I am a total zombie. So being a morning person myself, I had no problem getting up to check on Justin. By the way, my wife had already gotten up to start cooking our noon meal.

As I looked out the front door, I saw Justin standing at the end of the driveway where it met the dirt road. I am thinking, "Son, you are only ten feet from the mailbox, get the paper and come on."

Then I noticed a piece of paper taped to my front door. I really didn't want to let the cold air in but I needed to yell for him to come on and besides, the paper taped to my front door had my curiosity up. I opened the door and looked at the paper on my door. It was a note addressed to Granny Jean from Justin. The note read "Welcome back, Granny Jean."

I looked across the yard and there was Justin, all bundled up in his heavy clothes, looking down the dirt road waiting for Granny Jean to arrive. Terri and I could not believe it. We quietly closed the door and left him alone.

We continued getting ready, taking baths and whatnot, when we heard the front door slam again. Justin had gotten cold. He warmed by the fire and we fed him breakfast. Then he went out again to the dirt road. A little while later, he came back in from the cold but after getting warm, he went to his bedroom and opened the shades. He set up his toys to play so he could look out the window, hoping not to miss her when she arrived.

Titus 2:11-13, reads, "For the grace of God that brings salvation has appeared to all men, teaching us that, denying ungodliness and worldly lust, we should live soberly, righteously and godly in the present age, looking for the blessed hope and glorious appearing of our great God and Savior Jesus Christ…"

Friend, be honest to this next question: Are you standing by the dirt road looking for our Savior or are you so caught up in worldly lust, that you are distracted?

Friend, I challenge you to live in this world with a goal to honor God, but always with your eyes glancing in eager expectation towards the dirt road…He is coming again!!!

Hidden Corrosion

I am so blessed and thankful to have several automobiles. Growing up, we only had one as a family and normally it was gone, for Dad drove it to work. You know one good thing about having only one car? It keeps the family at home a lot. I do realize many people, like my family growing up, may not have this luxury. But, it can be a blessing to jump in the car, turn the key and go down the road.

Well, it's a blessing until you jump in your car, turn the key and it doesn't start. Now this is what I call an aggravating blessing. Next thing you know, you are standing in front of the car with the hood up staring at the engine with that "deer in the headlights" look.

Who in the world, what kind of engineers design these things? When you lift the hood on a car today, you immediately think, "I know there is an engine down here somewhere."

Not too long ago, I jumped in my car and turned the key...nothing. Nothing happened, except that feeling of just being punched in the gut. At this point, I wanted to do like my brother did as a teenager. Once when his truck wouldn't start, which for this truck happened often, he got out and left the hood closed. He then reached over in the back of the truck and brought out a pitchfork, and he began to beat the hood of the truck. I cannot say this fixed the truck and would not recommend it, but oh my, what a belly laugh I had. The truck still did not start but I think he felt better.

Anyway, I do know a little, notice I said a little, about cars and with my engine not even turning over, I thought it must have a dead battery. After checking it a couple of times, I found my battery was good and charged. The problem was that the terminal had corroded under the red plastic protector and didn't have a good connection. My whole problem was simple. Corrosion has created a separation between the cable and the battery, causing the battery to be ineffective.

As we read in Isaiah 59:2, we find a very similar problem between us and God, "But your iniquities (sins) have separated you from your God; And your sins have hidden His face from you, So that He will not hear."

Friend, do not miss this. <u>Sin is the corrosion that separates us from God!!!</u> God is Holy and will not tolerate sin. It does not matter what you think about your sin. You may say, "Well, I have never done…" or you may say, "What I did is not as bad as…" but hear what God's word says. Your sin, no matter how big or small to you, has already created separation between you and God and rendered <u>you</u> ineffective. So let me ask you, does your terminal need cleaning? Has corrosion slowly built up in your life?

God's word says, "If we confess our sin God is just and willing to forgive our sin." Confession means to agree with God about our actions and to not turn from those actions and behaviors means you really don't agree with God.

Friend, How can we knowingly have corrosion and do nothing about it? To do this means you really don't care about being connected to the battery. What can wash away my sin? Nothing but the blood of Jesus! What can make me whole again? Nothing but the blood of Jesus!

Happy Birthday

Have you ever been out to eat and a group of waiters and waitresses came out of the kitchen clapping and singing a 'happy birthday' song? This may have happened to you.

I like to watch what happens. Immediately everyone in the place stops eating, talking or reading the menu to see who is having a birthday (except for that rude person sitting next to you talking so loud on their cell phone that everyone in the place can hear).

You can normally tell who is having the birthday because they have a surprised look on their faces and they begin to slowly slide down in their seat. My wife and I were out enjoying a wonderful meal when I noticed my cousin and her husband walk in. Terri and I were sitting in a side room as we watched the waitress direct them to a table.

Now I was brought up to believe I should make the most of every opportunity. So, how could I waste this perfect opportunity? Shortly after they had sat down, our waitress came by and I pointed out my cousin and her husband at their table. I told her they were celebrating her birthday and could they possibly sing 'Happy Birthday' to her (which it really wasn't her birthday).

Terri and I enjoyed a wonderfully exciting, meal while we watched my cousin and her husband enjoy theirs. Next thing you know, out from the kitchen area, you hear it. A mass mob of waiters and waitresses proceed across the room clapping their hands and singing very loud, (This is great! We can't hear the person next to us talking on their cell phone). As people stopped what they were doing and looked, so did my cousin and her husband. The singing mob approached their table and stopped but the singing continued.

We had a great view of the whole party, from the side room where we were seated. They placed a piece of cake in front of my cousin as the happy birthday song is being belted out. I can see my cousin, once she got over the shock, mouthing over and over the words "It's not my birthday." The singing mob never missed a beat. My wife and I are in tears while my cousin and her husband are bouncing in and out of a state of shock.

In Matthew 7:21-23, Jesus says these words, "Not everyone who says to Me, Lord, Lord shall enter the kingdom of heaven, but he who does the will of my Father in heaven. Many will say to Me in that day, Lord, Lord have we not prophesied in Your name, cast out demons in Your name, and done many wonders in Your name? And then I will declare to them, I never knew you; depart from Me, you who practice lawlessness."

Friend, this is a sobering passage, for in the end, many people will be shocked and surprised. And why? Don't they seem to be doing many good things? Don't they seem to be doing things in the name of Jesus? Shouldn't this count for something? And God will answer, "I do not know you."

Friend, people try to please God in their own way and out of their own ideas, instead of reading, studying and following the truths of His word. In other words, many people try making the word of God fit their thoughts or ideas. We must be careful to make sure our thoughts and ideas about God align with the word of God.

Tractor Trailer

So, I was driving to work one morning about 5:30 down the Interstate. I noticed lights in my rearview mirror and they were gaining on me. The lights were tall and shining down into my car, then I realized it was a tractor-trailer.

The truck eased right up to my bumper and I heard the roar of the big diesel engine. The driver pulled out to pass me. I could see the shiny chrome bumper from the side window of my car. As the truck driver sped along the side of my car, I could see this was a newer model truck. You could tell the driver took care of the tractor-trailer truck. It had lights and chrome everywhere. It even had a custom paint job, chrome exhaust, sleeper cab and chrome wheels. As the trailer started coming beside me, I could tell it too was nice with lights all over it. The truck was so nice, I was even proud for the driver.

And then it hit me! I am serious, it hit me! No, no, not the truck. The awful smell hit me. You know, one of those smells that takes your breath and has you holding what breath you have left. The smell was so strong I could almost taste it. It made me want to spit. It so happened that as this beautiful tractor-trailer passed me, it was carrying hogs. Ripe ones!!!

Then it hit me again! No, no, not the smell, but a thought. I began to ask myself, "Am I ever like this?" As I drive down the road of life, do I look great to the people around me but as I pass by, do I leave a stench of ungodliness? Is there a foul smell of self-righteousness, pride or self-indulgence surrounding me?

In Matthew 23:25-28, Jesus said, "Woe to you scribes and Pharisees, hypocrites! For you cleanse the outside of the cup and dish, but inside they are full of extortion and self-indulgence. Blind Pharisee, first cleanse the inside of the cup and dish, that the outside of them may be clean also. Woe to you, scribes and Pharisees, hypocrites! For you are like whitewashed tombs which indeed appear beautiful outwardly, but inside are full of dead men's bones and all uncleanness. Even so you also outwardly appear righteous to men, but inside you are full of hypocrisy and lawlessness."

Are people glad to see me go or does my passing leave a fresh fragrance of someone who is real with God? Friend, we need to be honest with ourselves and answer these kinds of questions. For if the truth be known, when we pass people, we often tend to leave a little rottenness, decay and stench. And as for me, I can easily fall back to this, for I spent twenty years without Christ, passing on the rottenness, decay and stench in my life.

Friend, it's time to do a little cleaning on the inside of the cup. Pray that God will cleanse you from the inside out. This I promise; you can't hide it and cover it up, for eventually someone will smell what's on the inside.

Seashells

Terri, my wife really enjoys going to the beach and so do I. There's something about the sand, the sun, the smell of salt and the sound of the waves crashing onto the beach that relaxes and refreshes her.

I enjoy watching my boys chase crabs, dig holes and make sandcastles. The part my sons do not enjoy is the suntan lotion. I strip them down before we go to the beach and then cover them head to toe with lotion. Each day I repeat the process and out to the beach we go.

And no trip to the beach would be complete without a bucket and shovel. How can you fill the moat around the castle without a bucket? And what will you carry all those seashells in? I can see Terri and our two boys walking up the beach, picking up shells and coming back with a bucketful. Of course, I would have to look at the perfect shell they each had found. What wonderful memories.

Why am I packing this car? Didn't we just get here? Has a week gone by already? Why doesn't the time at work pass this quickly? All these thoughts come to mind while preparing to go home.

Goodbye beach, Goodbye water, Goodbye motel, Goodbye pool. As kids, you have to tell everything goodbye.

So the drive home begins and already my mind is beginning to get back into the "got to get it done mentality." When we get home, I need to wash the sand off all the chairs and let them dry. I need to unpack and put up all the stuff. Why did we take so much? And here is that bucket of shells.

Why did we bring another full bucket of shells home? We have to have them, don't you remember? Oh yeah! What shall I do with them? I know, I will place them next to the bucket of shells from last year; which is next to the bucket from the year before, which is next to the bucket from the year

91

before that, and so on it goes…you get the picture! Year after year, we have to bring home shells but never do anything with them.

In I John 1:5-6, we find these words from the Apostle John, "This is the message which we have heard from Him (Jesus) and declare to you, that God is light and in Him there is no darkness at all. If we say we have fellowship with Him (God) and walk in darkness, we lie and _do not practice the truth._"

Also in I John 2:5, we read the following, "But _whoever keeps_ His (Jesus) word, truly the love of God is perfected in him. By this we know that we are in Him."

Friend, don't miss the point here. Many people sit in churches year after year hungering for the truth, which is a great thing. Yet, year after year, they fail to do anything with the truth. For too long, the church has collected truth like my wife collects seashells and has failed to be productive with it. To know doctrinal truth for the sake of knowing doctrinal truth is missing the point.

Friend, we need to learn these truths so that we can apply them to our lives. We need to let God transform our lives through these truths and in doing so draw nearer to the heart of God! To live in such a way is to please Him! To Glorify Him!

Friend, let me offer a suggestion. Head on over to the bucket of truth that you have set next to last years bucket of truth, then knock off the dust they have collected, then dig through them and find one truth. Take that one truth and start applying it to your life.

Friend, start letting God use the truths you learn to build your life to His Glory!

First Day Of School

Years ago, my wife gave up her career to homeschool our boys. Let me say up front, homeschooling is not for every family but it was for ours. My wife did a wonderful job homeschooling our boys. Our school consisted of Terri, who was the teacher, Mitchell and Justin, who were the students. I am a very intelligent man and know my place so I would sit next to my boys for remedial classes.

Do you think I am kidding? Actually, I stayed out of the way. My role was the Principal, Headmaster or Big Chief, whatever title you prefer. Okay here is the truth; my role was to make sure my children respected their mother because I knew if they did not respect her, there would have been no home school.

It was <u>not</u> a good thing to have Mom call Dad at work because there was a behavior issue. I remember telling my wife to put them on the phone and I could hear them in the background saying, "No Mama, please don't make me talk to Dad." Come to think about it, to this day they still don't want to talk to me on the phone…I wonder why?

Anyway, when my oldest son, Mitchell, was in the eighth grade, we knew he was ready for public school. Mitchell played sports and had many friends at church that were attending the local public school. So we enrolled Mitchell in the public school as a freshman.

You ask, "Were you nervous?" Are you kidding… he was only going from a school of two to a school of 1800+ and he would have an army of teachers. Terri and I had tremendous reservations about this move.

Apparently, Terri and I were not the only ones having butterflies. Mitchell was concerned as well, until the morning before school started. Mitchell had been reading his bible and the verse for that day was found in Acts 2:25-26. Paul reminds us, of the words of King David concerning our God, "I foresaw the Lord always before my face, for <u>He is at my right hand, that I may not be shaken</u>. Therefore my heart rejoiced, and my tongue was glad; Moreover my flesh also will rest in hope."

Friend, God through His word calmed my son and assured him that God would surely be with him. When Mitchell shared this with Terri and me, we too were set at ease, knowing God had put Mitchell at ease.

How often we find ourselves in some sort of struggle or situation when we have allowed worry and anxiety to rule our thought life. This can get so bad that it begins to affect our sleep habits and even our health. And why? Because we fail to spend time with God in His word and gain our comfort from Him.

Friend, we seek comfort and advice in everything and from everyone but the one who can provide it. How foolish can we be? Wise, godly counsel is very important and has its role but counsel from God's word is vital. Counsel from God's word has no substitute!

Friend, if you are His child, God is with you! So, no matter the situation you may be facing right now, you should have one main goal. To glorify God in it!!! And how can we glorify him if we don't get comfort and direction from His word.

At the time of this writing, my son has been offered a scholarship to play baseball at a private college. The scholarship covers one-half of the tuition. This sounds great but the tuition is very expensive. Having no college savings, we are on the pay-as-you-go-plan and this becomes a very big financial decision.

I have called several friends of mine to seek their advice. I have talked with his coach. I have talked with my accountability partner, who is a high school baseball coach. I have talked with several coworkers. I have talked with my family and my wife. At this point I had no comfort in this decision.

But while waiting for my wife to get home, I went back to writing this short story and it dawned on me...whom have I forgotten to ask? No wonder I have no comfort in this decision. I have forgotten to ask God, through His word and through prayer!

Think I will go now...there is someone I need to talk with.

Sacrifice Bunt

Mitchell, my oldest son, plays baseball. I did not grow up playing sports but I really enjoy watching my son play ball. And I really enjoy baseball because it is a team sport that teaches him to work with others. It forces him to celebrate the strengths of his fellow players. Since he is a pitcher, he has to rely on the strengths of the other players to make him look good. I would guess one of the hardest jobs of a coach is to get a group of players to work and think as one.

One thing I have learned is that if I have the attitude that my son should be playing instead of some other kid and I let my son hear me say this, it would be counter-productive in team unity. My son might cop an attitude towards some other player and we know many talented teams that have been beaten because of this attitude.

I have tried to teach my son that you may not agree with a coach's decision but it's not like they are trying to make decisions so they can lose the game. I told him, "They have a plan and you may not like the plan, but it's okay, just go with it." Sometimes it's hard to get kids to understand this concept and it's always hard to get us bench-coaching parents to understand.

Let me give you an example of what I am trying to say. I was watching one of my son's games and my son's team was up to bat. They had 2 guys on base, a man on first and a man on second with no outs. Now what is typically going through a kid's mind in this situation? "I got to get a hit!" and or "I have at least got to get on base!"

Now what is typically going through a parent's mind? "I hope he hits a home run!" (This is me.) But, if you are a student of the game or a coach, you are most likely thinking a ground ball hit could be a double play and we could have at least 2 outs. A better option would be to play small ball and have the batter sacrifice bunt. This would end up with one out but possibly move the 2 runners in scoring position and out of a double-play situation.

Mitchell's coach signals for a bunt and Mitchell steps up to bat. The pitcher throws the ball and Mitchell turns to bunt but tries to drag bunt. This is where the batter will turn to run while trying to bunt, hoping to lay down a bunt and also make it safely to first. Instead a foul ball and strike one is called. The coach signals for another bunt and Mitchell tries to drag bunt again. "Foul ball, strike two" the umpire calls.

Now there is a problem. If he bunts on third strike and fouls the ball off, it is an automatic out. So the coach signals for Mitchell to hit and this is a lot of pressure, since he is behind in the count. The pitcher throws the ball. Mitchell swings and I can see it going over the fence... well not exactly. It's a swing and a miss, "strike three," the umpire calls. My son is out and the runners do not advance. My boy turned around, his head down, and walked back to the dugout and now his team has one out with men still in a double play situation.

Why? Why did this happen? I believe it happened because my son did not really understand what "sacrifice bunt" really meant.

In Romans 12:1-2 we read, "I beseech you therefore brethren, by the mercies of God, that you present your bodies a living sacrifice, holy, acceptable to God, which is your reasonable service. And do not be conformed to this world, but be transformed by the renewing of your mind, that you may prove what is that good and acceptable and perfect will of God."

Friend, my son let his team down because unknowingly, he was selfish. He wanted to help his team but he did not want to sacrifice himself in the process. In other words, he was more concerned about himself than the team.

And here lies the problem. We live in a world where "sacrifice" is not the norm, but "self" is. You know exactly what I am saying and exactly what my son struggled with…because you struggle with the same thing. But friend, knowing the sacrifice God endured for you and me, how can we not sacrifice for Him?

In Romans, we just read sacrifice is reasonable. Friend, <u>for a child of God, a sacrificial life should be the norm.</u> We have got to understand that our mentality of "I will love God as long as I don't have to _____" (Fill in the blank) is not really a love for God; it's a love for our own self.

Friend, this is how the world thinks and verse two says we are not to be conformed to the world. This mentality places us before God, which at its core is idol worship.

Friend, do not put this book down without thinking about this. Is there an area of your life where you have placed yourself first and God second? Be Honest with yourself. Think about it.

Now do something about it!!!

The Pool

Growing up in rural Georgia, my favorite time of the year was summer when my cousins would come to stay with us. We would roam the woods and fields playing, swimming, fishing, picking blackberries and plums, which was followed by some good old scratching. You have to scratch the chiggers that you got picking blackberries. Sometimes our legs looked like we were shot with bird shot from all the chigger bites.

We also did what bored country boys do; we tried chewing rabbit tobacco. Sometimes we used notebook paper to roll it up in and then tried to smoke it. That stuff would make you green at the gills. That means sick as a dog for you cultured readers.

My favorite time was hanging out at the creek; it always seemed to be cooler at the creek. Besides, we would skinny-dip in the creek, if there were no girls around. We actually had a swimming hole that was a deep part of the creek. We would clean it out before we swam. We would remove all the sticks and debris from the sandy bottom. What a perfect place.

The creek had tall trees that not only provided shade but also one tree provided the perfect Tarzan vine. My older brothers and cousins found a natural vine and cut it at the ground so we could swing out over the water and drop in. This worked great until my mom... who has always been a daredevil; decided she would try it. Out over the water she swung until she and the Tarzan vine came crashing to the water. Game over; let's go home! Bummer!!!

I remember Dad bringing home a big fat rope. My brothers hung it in the tree and we were back in business. We thought we were in high cotton with our new Tarzan vine...Tarzan had nothing on us!!!

When I was a boy, people did not have pools in their back yards like they do today. I remember only 2 families that even had cement ponds; as Jethro, from the Beverly Hillbillies would say. So the creek or a regular fish pond is where people would swim.

Today it's different. Many people I know have pools. One good friend of mine had just built a pool and invited us over for a swim. Only Justin, my youngest son, and I could go. Their cement pond had salt water in it which is very different than I was used to. In fact, I found it to be very enjoyable and refreshing. Of course when it's July in Georgia and old Mr. Sun is bearing down, a cool dip is always enjoyable.

Now, my friend had no Tarzan vine in his cement pond and come to think of it, I believe a Tarzan vine wouldn't have fit in with salt water. I don't ever remember Tarzan at the beach.

Anyway, we had a great time and on the way home, Justin asked, "Dad, don't you want a cold Icee from the store?" Now what he was really saying is, "Dad could you buy me an Icee at the store?" But I played the game and said, "Sure I want one." So, off to the store we drove.

As we were driving, we passed a house with a pool. Justin said, "Look Dad, they still have the cover on it." Sure enough, he was right. I thought, it's Georgia in the middle of July and they still have the cover on the pool. But I told him they probably had a good reason why their pool is covered and closed.

Friend, many people treat God's word like those people treated their pool...Closed!!!

In their mind, they have a good reason to keep the cover on God's word closed. There are millions of reasons and excuses we make up as to why our bibles stay covered and closed. But friend, there are no good reasons. Friend, we cannot honestly say anything that will justify the neglect of God's word.

As a child of God, His Word is vital to us no matter if we believe it or not. I want you to read just a few verses from one chapter in the book of Psalms:

- The Psalmist writes in Psalm 119:50, "This is my comfort in my affliction, For Your (Gods) word has given me life." See how the Psalmist knows that God's word is a comfort in troubled times. Friend, where do you turn in times of trouble?

- Psalm 119:72, "The law of Your (God's) mouth is better to me than thousands of shekels of gold and silver." Friend, is God's word more important to you than money and material possessions?

- Psalm 119:103, "How sweet are Your words to my taste, Sweeter than honey to my mouth!" Friend, is God's word sweeter to you than any dessert the best bakers in the world can dream up? Do you have a sweet tooth for His word?

- Psalm 119:105, "Your word is a lamp to my feet and a light to my path." Friend, is God's word the light that guides your steps or are you stumbling in the darkness?

Friend, just as a pool will not refresh and revive you unless it's cover is opened, so God's word will not unless you open its cover. Maybe it's time for you and I to open it up and dive in.

The Gunsmith

I was talking with a friend of mine, Johnny. We were talking about our favorite guns to hunt with. I began to tell him about a pump shotgun that I really enjoyed shooting. He was telling me about a favorite pump shotgun of his that he hunted with for many years.

Johnny knew his shotgun needed a thorough cleaning, so he set aside some time one day to clean it. Johnny began to tell me how he carefully disassembled it piece by piece. As he removed each part, he cleaned it and set it aside. Eventually, he had the pump shotgun completely apart and each part cleaned and oiled.

As Johnny continued to tell his story, it became very humorous when he began to describe the reassembly process. In fact, he decided to rest for the day…in other words, he had gotten aggravated with it. Over a period of weeks, he would tackle this project again and again.

Finally it happened. You know what I am talking about, when things click for you. Well, it clicked for Johnny; he finally put all the parts in a box and began looking for a gunsmith. It clicked for Johnny because he finally gave up.

I wish I could write the story as he told it because at this point, I was in stitches. Now, admitting failure for Johnny was not easy. It was especially difficult since he was a mechanic and not only that, he had advanced to a mechanical supervisor.

Maybe it's true, they promote people who don't know how to do anything. I don't know, just thinking out loud here. Friend, you don't happen to be a supervisor do you??? (Just kidding)

Anyway, Johnny told me about visiting the gunsmith. He opened the door of the gunsmith business and stepped in with his box of loose gun parts tucked under his arm. As

Johnny placed the box on the counter, he greeted the guy. Then as he slid the box across the counter towards the gunsmith, he began to tell his dilemma. The gunsmith chuckled and replied, "You are not the first person to have this problem."

Friend, did you get it??? You can spend all the time you have trying to get your life together, but you never will. All we can do is mess it up! Friend, we are in a terrible dilemma.

Paul addresses this terrible dilemma we are in, in the book of Romans, chapter 7. Take time to read and study it. Now in verse 15 he says, "For what I am doing I do not understand. For what I will to do that I do not practice: but what I hate, that I do."

In verse 24, Paul admits he is in a terrible hopeless condition, "O wretched man that I am!" Then he continues with a question, "Who will deliver me from this body of death?"

Paul admits he is wretched (sinful) and in a situation he cannot fix. But he doesn't leave us there. Paul gives us the solution to the problem. It's found in verse 25, "I thank God through Jesus Christ our Lord!"

Friend, your life may be in shambles or there may be an area of your life that you have totally messed up. And friend, it will never be fixed…until you stand at the counter with God. Friend, you must admit you are wretched and hopeless, then slide your box of brokenness and despair across the counter towards Him. Friend you won't be the first!!!

Broken, messed-up lives are all we have to offer Him but the good news is that He is in the business of fixing our brokenness. Just let Him have it!

What A Plane Ride

Justin, my youngest son, is a very artistic. My wife and I can't even draw stick men Go figure. Justin's passion is cartoons and he can quote the history about cartoons and the animators who draw them. When he sees cartoons, he sees things you and I just don't see. If you are artistic, you know what I mean.

One August, several years back, our paper featured an article on a local man who was a Christian Cartoonist. Todd, had began as a graphic designer and then started a ministry called, Timbucktoons. Todd's ministry provides materials, videos and such to churches for their children's programs. I kept the article and showed it to Justin.

Justin said, "Dad I want to meet this guy." I responded, "Okay." But, each time I thought about calling Todd, I felt uncomfortable, which is not like me at all.

August turned to September and before you know it I was working a shutdown at my job. This meant working six twelve-hour shifts, for about four to six weeks.

Then in November, my company asked me to travel to New Jersey. A few of us were tasked with performing an acceptance test on a piece of equipment the company was purchasing. I agreed and we began purchasing our plane tickets. I informed my boss that at the end of the week, I needed to fly from New Jersey to Kansas City for a previously planned trip. The second week of November each year was when I went pheasant hunting with my dad.

If I had flown back home from New Jersey first, I would not have arrived in time to travel with my dad and several other men. They were traveling by truck to carry the dogs, guns, shells and such. If I could fly directly to Kansas City, I could meet them at the hunting store, where we usually stopped to buy our hunting license and stretch our legs.

My company said they would not pay the several hundred dollars for a one-way ticket for me to go from New Jersey to Kansas City. This really angered me. Here I am willing to travel to New Jersey, in November, to check out their equipment. Come on people!!! It's not like several hundred dollars will break a humongous company. It's not like I am asking to fly to Hawaii. Oh brother!!!

Well, I started looking for airline tickets. I finally found a flight that would fly me from New Jersey to Atlanta, then to Kansas City. It was with the same carrier and my flight was actually cheaper than a round trip ticket from the city near where I live.

It sounded good to me, but it put me in Kansas City much later than I wanted. I would have to catch a cab from the airport and drive another hour or so to get to the hunting store. I didn't want Dad and the guys waiting on me and I knew I would be pushing it. But, the extra money for the direct flight was a large amount to me, so I went to Kansas City through Atlanta.

I made it to New Jersey. We checked out the equipment and on Friday of that week, I was sitting in the Newark, New Jersey airport, waiting on my plane. All of a sudden, my cell phone rang. It was my older brother, John.

He said, "Phillip, I am praying for you today. What do you need me to pray about?" I told him I had to fly to Atlanta, then to Kansas City and then rent a cab or somehow get to the hunting store. I told him that I did not need luggage problems, plane delays or travel problems. John began to pray for me. As we hung up I thought what a blessing it is to have godly brothers…and parents!!!

The flight to Atlanta was okay, but the flight from Atlanta to Kansas City was phenomenal. When I got on the plane in Atlanta, I sat next to the window. A guy came and sat next to me. I started the conversation.

108

"Hello, I am Phillip."
"I am Charlie." We shook hands.
"Where are you from Charlie? "
"The Tampa Bay/Clearwater area of Florida."
"What do you do there?"
"I have a Christian ministry to Children called "Uncle Charlie.""
"What do you do?"
"I travel to churches and lead in children's worship, provide worship kits, DVD's and such."
"Awesome, I too am a Christian."
"Wonderful, where are you from?"
"I live near Augusta, Georgia."
"No Kidding...I have a very good friend who lives in Augusta. He is a cartoonist and edits some of my material."

Friend, I had totally forgotten about the article in the newspaper back home and my son wanting to visit the guy. In fact, I could not even remember his name, so I didn't bring it up. I did tell Charlie my son loves cartooning and talked of being a cartoonist. Charlie said, "Your son needs to meet my friend. Here is his phone number, website, and address, give him a call." When I got home, the name Charlie gave me was the exact person who was featured in the newspaper. WOW!!!

I called Todd and he told me Charlie had already called and told him I would be getting in touch with him. So Justin and I went to meet him. They talked about stuff of which I had no clue.

But here is the cool thing. Before we left Todd said, "Justin, I want to do something for you." Todd reached over put his hand on Justin's shoulder and began to pray over him.

Friend, I had tears in my eyes, thinking how Awesome God truly is.

Back to the Plane Ride:

So, my plane is about to land. Charlie and I had some wonderful conversation and fellowship. He asked where I was going pheasant hunting and I asked where the church was he going to. He mentioned some town in Kansas and then he said, "All I know is, I take Interstate 435 South and then take Interstate 70 West and then drive about 2 hours.

I could not believe what I was hearing. I said, "Charlie, I need to be at the junction of 435 South and 70 West. Charlie had a car rented and waiting and was more than happy to drop me off at the front door of the hunting store. Friend, I was there about 3 minutes after my dad and the other guys arrived. What a great trip! What a great God!

I was angry because things did not work out the way I wanted. But if I had gotten what I wanted, I would have never met Charlie, Justin would have most likely not met Todd, I would have had to find my own transportation to the hunting store, and my brother would not have seen God answer his prayer.

Who would have dreamed to put all this together, but God? I know some people are skeptical and say it was a coincidence; but I know it was God, once again proving to me that He is Real and For Real.

Open My Eyes And Let Me See!!!

Everyone Has A "Story"

In conclusion, I challenge you to let God "open your eyes and let you see." These stories are based on my life. What is it that God wants you to "write down" about your life?

I hope that this book will inspire you to see things differently than before. It is true that "everyone has a story" but most people have more than one story to tell. If you think back, you may remember things that happened in your past that revealed God to you: answers to prayers, safety in a serious situation, intervening in circumstances, providing a need, etc. Keeping a journal of events will cause you to look back with thanks and praise to Him but will also give you the faith to trust Him more in your everyday life.

As you read and study God's word, stay focused on Him and ask Him to give you a hungering to know Him better and to live for Him. Remember, it's not about you; it's about Him.

So, take out your bible, a notebook, get alone with God and begin to write. May God Bless You!

I welcome your comments regarding this book. You can reach me by email: *pjknox@phillipknox.net*

Acknowledgements

Often in life, God sends people across our path as springboards to propel us in our Christian walk. I have been blessed to have had many such people in my life. I would much prefer not to mention anyone, for I know I will forget someone. Nevertheless, with deep love and appreciation to all, I will try to limit my thanks.

Mom and Dad, you are the most real Christians I know. You live it out!!! Terri you are a true southern belle, a humble, godly woman and wonderful wife... I am so undeserving!!! Mitchell and Justin, it is a joy to see God working in your lives. Thanks for living and listening to my stories over and over and <u>over</u>.

To each person in these stories, God has used you to help open my eyes. Thank You!

Hal Rowland, your words of encouragement were like rain to my parched, July garden! Thank You!

Karen McGowan, God is always on time, and so were you! Thank you for giving me the gentle nudges to move forward and for paving my path by writing your book "Faith to Finish".

Paul McGowan, the cover is fantastic. It's me. Thank You!

Steve Hartman, Thank you for making sure I am handling the word of God correctly.

Bill Whaley, You are the computer guru.

Melba Dismuke, For the untold hours you poured into this book and for your loving patience with me, the words "Thank You" just don't seem to do justice.

To my Lord, Jesus Christ, It is with tears in my eyes I write of your love for me. Thank you for letting me have eyes to see...and ears to hear!!!!!!

To schedule a speaking engagement
or for book information contact:
Phillip J Knox

Email:philknox@bellsouth.net